GOLDSMITHS, SILVERSMITHS AND BANKERS:

Innovation and the Transfer of Skill, 1550 to 1750

A collection of working papers given at a study day held jointly by the Centre for Metropolitan History and the Victoria and Albert Museum, 24 November 1993

Edited by

David Mitchell

Centre for Metropolitan History
Working Papers Series, No. 2

Published by
Alan Sutton Publishing Limited
and
Centre for Metropolitan History

1995

First published in the United Kingdom in 1995 by
Alan Sutton Publishing Limited
Phoenix Mill · Far Thrupp · Stroud · Gloucestershire
and
Centre for Metropolitan History
Institute of Historical Research · School of Advanced Study · University of London
Senate House · Malet Street · London WC1E

Copyright © the authors 1995

All rights reserved. No part of this publication may be reproduced, stored in a retrieval system, or transmitted, in any form or by any means, electronic, mechanical, photocopying, recording or otherwise, without the prior permission of the publishers and copyright holder[s].

British Library Cataloguing in Publication Data

A catalogue record for this book is available from the British Library.

ISBN 0 7509 0908 0

Cover illustration:
Lid of comb box with Venus and Adonis from the Calverley toilet service
with the mark of William Fowle, London 1683–4.
Silver (24.4 cm x 18.7 cm; weight 60 oz 5 dwt).
(*Victoria and Albert Museum*)

Produced by Alan Sutton Publishing Ltd.
Printed in Great Britain by The Alden Press Ltd., Oxford and Northampton

TO ARTHUR GRIMWADE
who first raised a number of the questions
discussed in these papers and who by his
learning, enthusiasm and kindness is a
constant encouragement to younger scholars.

Invitation to dine at Goldsmiths' Hall, showing a panorama of
craft operations, 1701/2. (Detail)
(*Worshipful Company of Goldsmiths*)

Contents

Preface	vii
Notes on Contributors	viii
Introduction PHILIPPA GLANVILLE	1
Innovation and the transfer of skill in the goldsmiths' trade in Restoration London DAVID MITCHELL	5
Goldsmiths' apprenticeship during the first half of the seventeenth century: the situation in Paris MICHÈLE BIMBENET-PRIVAT	23
Training and workshop practice in Zürich in the seventeenth century HANSPETER LANZ	32
Aliens and their impact on the goldsmiths' craft in London in the sixteenth century LIEN BICH LUU	43
Balances and goldsmith-bankers: the co-ordination and control of inter-banker debt clearing in seventeenth-century London STEPHEN QUINN	53
The interaction between English and Huguenot goldsmiths in the late seventeenth and early eighteenth centuries EMMA PACKER	77
'The King's Arms and Feathers'. A case study exploring the networks of manufacture operating in the London goldsmiths' trade in the eighteenth century HELEN CLIFFORD	84
The design of London goldsmiths' shops in the early eighteenth century CLAIRE WALSH	96
The goldsmiths and the London luxury trades, 1550 to 1750 JOHN STYLES	112

Preface

The following essays originated as papers given at an international study day held on 24 November 1993 at the Victoria and Albert Museum. John Styles, of the Victoria and Albert Museum/Royal College of Art M.A. programme, and I jointly organised the event which was intended to promote the discussion of themes explored in 'The development of the skilled workforce in London, 1500–1750', a project based at the Centre for Metropolitan History. The study day examined innovation and skill in the goldsmiths' trade. Themes included the education and training of apprentices, workshop equipment and practice, and the role of immigrants as agents of change in technique and design. Participants came from different disciplines and included economic and design historians, archivists and librarians, curators and collectors, dealers and auctioneers.

This book is the fruit of the co-operative efforts of several individuals and institutions. Thanks are owed to many: to Philippa Glanville and John Styles at the Victoria and Albert Museum, who were instrumental in arranging the study day; to Gerry Martin of the Renaissance Trust and Brand Inglis of Tessiers Ltd., whose generosity enabled foreign participants to be invited; to all the speakers who stuck nobly to their given briefs, and to the lively audience who made the event so stimulating; to the Goldsmiths' Company, the South Square Trust and Tessiers Ltd., whose grants have made possible the publication of this book; to Olwen Myhill for her skill and patience in typesetting the volume; to my colleagues of the Skilled Workforce project for their advice and forbearance; and finally, to my wife Shirin who, despite her misgivings as to my editorial skill in view of my eccentric grasp of punctuation, has been a constant encouragement.

David Mitchell
Centre for Metropolitan History
Institute of Historical Research
School of Advanced Study
University of London

December 1994

Notes on Contributors

PHILIPPA GLANVILLE is Curator of the Department of Metalwork, Silver, and Jewellery at the Victoria and Albert Museum, London. She has written extensively on the history of English plate including *Silver in Tudor and Early Stuart England* (London, 1990).

DAVID MITCHELL is a member of the research team of the 'Skilled Workforce Project', funded by the Renaissance Trust, at the Centre for Metropolitan History, Institute of Historical Research, University of London. A major concern of the project is innovation and the transfer of skill in early modern London.

MICHÈLE BIMBENET-PRIVAT is a conservateur en chef at the Archives nationales, Paris. Her recent work includes a monograph on Parisian goldsmiths, *Les Orfèvres Parisiens de la Renaissance 1506–1620* (Paris, 1992).

HANSPETER LANZ is Curator of Silver at the Schweizerisches Landesmuseum, Zürich. He has written several articles on Zürich goldsmiths and prepared with others the catalogue of a major exhibition, *Barocker Luxus* (Zürich, 1988).

LIEN BICH LUU is preparing a doctoral thesis, 'Skills and Innovations: a study of the role of the stranger working community in London *c*. 1550–1600', at the Centre for Metropolitan History, Institute of Historical Research, University of London.

STEPHEN QUINN is a visiting assistant professor at the College of William and Mary, Williamsburg, Virginia. He presented a doctoral thesis, 'Banking before the Bank: London's unregulated goldsmith-bankers, 1660-94', to the University of Illinois in 1994.

EMMA PACKER is an inventory clerk concerned with silver in the Royal Collection. She graduated from the V&A/RCA M.A. in the History of Design in 1992. Her dissertation was entitled 'Refining the Goldsmith: The London Goldsmiths' Trade seen through Inventories, 1695–1732'.

HELEN CLIFFORD is Leverhulme Research Fellow at the Ashmolean Museum, Oxford. She presented a doctoral thesis, 'Parker and Wakelin: the study of an eighteenth-century goldsmithing firm *c*. 1760–6, with particular reference to the Garrard Ledgers', to the Royal College of Art, London, in 1989.

CLAIRE WALSH is a lecturer at the Institute of Design, University of Teesside. She graduated from the V&A/RCA M.A. in the History of Design in 1993. Her dissertation was entitled 'Shop design and the display of goods in the eighteenth century'.

JOHN STYLES is Head of the V&A/RCA M.A. course in the History of Design. His writing includes 'Manufacturing, consumption and design in eighteenth-century England', in J. Brewer and R. Porter (eds.), *Consumption and the World of Goods* (London, 1993).

Introduction

PHILIPPA GLANVILLE

> The Goldsmith ought to be a good designer and have good Taste in Sculpture. He must be conversant in Alchemy; that is in all the Properties of metals:... He must know the various Ways of Essaying Metals, and distinguishing the real from the fictitious... he ought to be possessed of a solid Judgement as well as a mechanical Hand and Head. His Education, with respect to his Business, does not require to be very liberal; a plain English Education will suffice; Designing is the chief Part of his early Study, previous to his Apprenticeship.
>
> R. Campbell, *The London Tradesman* (1747)

As Campbell's guide to careers spells out, the qualifications for a successful career as a goldsmith were both diverse and specific. These essays explore aspects of the precious metals in London between 1500 and 1750. In that period London's population grew from about 50,000 to about 600,000 and the number of goldsmiths, already considered large by Italian visitors in the early Tudor period, had grown too. In 1773 some 800 signed a petition against the extension of the assay to Birmingham and Sheffield.

The subject is evolving rapidly in new directions and the papers pose new questions and explore new sources of information. The starting point is the nature of change, how and why London evolved from being around 1500 an importer of luxury manufactures in the precious metals — so that Cardinal Wolsey had to send to Bruges for candelabra and James I paid far more for Nuremburg plate than for the local product — to the mid eighteenth century when the rulers of Russia and Portuguese noblemen regularly placed orders with London goldsmiths. What were the gradual subtle shifts and innovations in practice, in technique, in attitude, in management of resources, in marketing, in metallurgy, even in religious, sexual or ethnic profile which, working together, engineered this transformation of the craft?

Mid nineteenth-century aesthetic theory idealised the handmade as against the power of the machine, an attitude which has largely coloured writings on silver until recently. Variations in facture and lack of uniformity were admired as evidence of the master's personal touch, his identity neatly guaranteed by his mark. Each object was taken as unique, there was little awareness of serial production and documents were selectively quoted for their picturesque details. The evidence of construction such as the repetition of stampings or cast elements and its implication for workshop practice was ignored, or underplayed. But objects can, and should trigger questions.

Answers to some questions are now emerging as documentary sources are scoured, objects assessed in groups or categories rather than singly, and the romantic personalization of the master goldsmith dissolves into the reality of the team of diverse specialists concerned with the production of plate, each with his or her particular skills, from refining to burnishing, from book-keeping to chasing.

An early example of scholarly groundwork is the analysis by Charles Oman of Elizabethan communion cups. Some 2,000 survive, the largest body of silver in Europe available for comparison apart from spoons. These cups were made as a result of a political decision for a particular purpose and to a more or less standard design in a brief period of less than twenty years by goldsmiths in every region of England; but they vary greatly. The first and largest class of silver to be catalogued (from the 1840s), these cups have also the advantage of a relatively rich documentary context. Working with the objects and the related Elizabethan churchwardens' accounts, Oman and other specialists identified both London and regional goldsmiths and exposed the emulation in Chester, Exeter and Norwich of the London assay system. The elaborate moresque bands engraved on London cups became a simplified crude 'dot and dash' on pieces made in Wales, Lincolnshire or Cumberland, a vivid reminder of the need for specialised skills and their lack away from the large concentrations of goldsmiths. The craft spanned an enormous spectrum of skill and customers ran from the Court to humble artisans.

Before the physical evidence can be exploited, a sustained attack is needed on large numbers of objects, measuring, weighing and comparing techniques of facture and decoration. As David Mitchell has pointed out, there can be genuine uncertainty as to how a particular effect was achieved, whether by casting or chasing, or commonly a mixture of the two; these highly specific facts are the key to craft practice, to the mysterious world of the workshop, and to identifying innovation in technique.

How these innovations arrived, who transmitted new ideas from where and the part played by alien goldsmiths are not new questions. But comparisons between the practices of the various European centres of goldsmithing, their contrasting attitudes to training and to the qualifications enabling a man to make and sell, the existence or lack of formal drawing schools are now being made for the first time.

When Nicholas Hilliard took himself to Paris in the 1570s, he hoped to acquire marketable skills available neither in his father's Exeter workshop nor in London. What he aspired to learn were the intangible qualities which gave Paris plate its distinctive appeal to the international market. But his was a rare example of enterprise for an English craftsman. The cross-Channel traffic was almost all one way, in the other direction.

The career of the Zürich goldsmith Dietrich Meyer described by Dr Lanz is unusual only in that his programme of self-improvement through an extended European tour can be documented. Between 1669 and 1674 his journeyman sketchbook records his work in Basel, Augsburg, Amsterdam and Basel again before his return to Zürich, armed with a novel series of motifs in the high baroque floral style — silver was a luxury product, subject to fashion and customers, particularly at the top of the market, expected and were prepared to pay for novelty of design in ornament, so the well-travelled journeyman, with good manual skills and the right connections, could interpret a new look. He may have brought home patterns for chasing; he did acquire sheets of engraved ornament. Whether he also acquired other equipment we do not know.

The constant rhetoric of complaint from English workmen against alien journeymen has absorbed much scholarly energy. From the standpoint of the client, their view was irrelevant; novelty was all. For the retailer, juggling his margins and manipulating credit, buying cheap and selling dear, was the key to success; skill in judging the alloy and organising a supply ready for working was essential. Again, the evidence is indirect.

Valuations of secondhand plate prepared by goldsmith-assessors show an ability to set widely varying price levels per ounce and the ability to distinguish and value foreign plate and coin. Sir Isaac Newton's alteration of the sterling standard in the interests of protecting the coinage and the London goldsmiths' apparently easy adaptation to the new higher standard indicate a degree of sophistication for which there was no formal training. But as Stephen Quinn's studies of early banking show, an understanding of bi-metallic balances was essential. A successful goldsmith had to be far more than a good craftsman, particularly one dealing more than casually with coin and bullion. An essential but intangible aspect of skill was a good address (in both senses), a reputation as a man of integrity and discretion, the right family network and marital opportunity, and access to customers.

Emma Packer has argued from the absence or presence of workshop equipment in her analysis of later seventeenth- and early eighteenth-century inventories to support her categorisations into retail goldsmith or working silversmith. The claim on eighteenth-century trade cards that plate was made on the premises was clearly in some cases a marketing device, a way of exploiting the customer's wish for a direct line to the maker in the interests of obtaining value for money. More significant as a means to secure sales were the layout, decoration and location of the retail premises, a theme explored by Claire Walsh.

Elaine Barr's biography of George Wickes (1980) shows the success of his policy of moving his shop to the West End and building up a wealthy aristocratic client list, as Thomas Folkingham had done before him. The retail business he created from the 1730s depended on his making a skilful balance between the demands for highly fashionable wares, designed by William Kent and others, and his ability to keep his team of chasers, modellers, casters and engravers in work. The bankruptcy in 1747 of his artistically more gifted contemporary, Paul Crespin, is a reminder of the need for commercial skills as well as originality.

The availability and use of handbooks, technical treatises, printed designs, moulds and patterns has been little studied in England. They leave little trace of their existence in inventories, although this apparent absence may be as much to do with the practices of the probate appraisers as with a real lack. When Peter Peterson, a Norwich goldsmith with a considerable business, specified the disposal of his lead patterns in his will in 1603, he was leaving an asset of real value which any goldsmith with a demanding clientele would have needed. But he is unusual in mentioning them. The inventory of the refiner Thomas Loveday, taken in 1682, was specific as to the (valuable) minerals, chemicals and colours in his refining house. Again, this full list is extremely unusual. Unlike the Paris goldsmiths' inventories published by Michèle Bimbenet-Privat, lists of tools and essential workshop equipment rarely occur in England. The fullest published list of workshop equipment is that of a Boston, Massachusetts, goldsmith, Richard Conyers, who had trained in London. Taken in 1709 by two goldsmith-appraisers, this inventory runs to 80 entries — a button stamp, nurling irons, swages, stamps, spoon punches, screw plates, brass patterns and so on.

The full list of Conyers' working materials is too early to include any reference to rolled sheet but the advent of the rolling mill early in the eighteenth century, presumably transformed the economics of production, although so far its impact has been assessed only in relation to the Sheffield plate industry. Analysis of the molecular structure of English hollow wares of, say, 1720 to 1750 would pin down the arrival of rolled sheet. A generation earlier, in the later seventeenth century, there was a burst of creative energy in the precious metals and apparently a transfer of technique (perhaps from the Mint) to the producers of spoons. Decorative raised motifs ('laceback') appear on both London and provincial spoons, struck using a die. Are these the 'spoon punches' listed in the 1709 Boston inventory?

The past thirty years have seen a transformation in silver studies. As far as London studies are concerned, since 1982 the longstanding tradition of object-focused research by collectors, auctioneers and curators has been cross-fertilised by the more theoretical approaches of the V&A/RCA History of Design course, refreshing the subject from diverse springs. Documents have been published or made available to researchers — the Returns of Aliens, the Sun Fire insurance policies, the Garrard ledgers. Computer technology has opened up large volumes of data for analysis such as the hearth tax and subsidy lists, object records in museums and makers' marks. Even without a computer, Arthur Grimwade's monumental biographical directory, first published in 1976 and now in its third, expanded edition is the essential starting point for serious silver research.

The expansion in postgraduate courses in the humanities since the 1970s produced the first crop of doctoral theses on aspects of the precious metals. Three scholars simultaneously investigated the specialised world of the chaser, the aristocrat of the goldsmith's workshop. Richard Edgecumbe's biographical directory of goldchasers in eighteenth-century England was awarded a D.Phil. in 1980, Dr Johan ter Molen produced a masterful study and exhibition on the Van Vianen family of Utrecht, Prague and London in 1984 and Heidi Prael-Himmer published a study of the Augsburg chaser Johann Andreas Thelot in 1978. Barbara Ward's Ph.D. analysing the careers of early Boston goldsmiths distinguished between retailers, embryo goldsmith-bankers and working silversmiths in Massachusetts. A Swedish scholar reconstructed the output of Erik Romer, active in London in the later eighteenth century, and Kenneth Quickenden explored the career of the entrepreneur Matthew Boulton. The latter was a contribution to business history as much as to silver studies, as is the Ph.D. thesis of Helen Clifford on the West End business of John Parker and Edward Wakelin.

The first full biography of an English goldsmith, Paul de Lamerie, was published over fifty years ago. In 1990 new insights, new documentary discoveries and a wholesale revision of assumptions (apart from some wonderful objects) enlivened Susan Hare's exhibition at Goldsmiths' Hall. The German goldsmith Wenzel Jamnitzer received the accolade of an exhibition at Nuremburg in 1985 and for almost all the major European goldsmithing centres biographical directories have been published in the past twenty-five years, a process in which the French have led the field.

In England, a specialist Silver Society with a journal and lecture programme has evolved from a dining club for collectors. Others now flourish in Washington, New York, Belgium, Holland and Germany, a focus for enthusiasts to exchange discoveries and elaborate on projects. The discipline of design history has illuminated the goldsmith's eclectic use of printed sources of ornament; Michael Snodin's exhibition *Rococo Art and Design in Hogarth's England* (V&A, 1984) demonstrated the power of the print as a medium for style for both goldsmith and patron and further undermined the 'heroic maker' model. In short, our subject is in energetic life, bubbling with ideas and questions, nurtured by the rich seedbed of two centuries of silver collecting and silver studies.

Innovation and the transfer of skill in the goldsmiths' trade in Restoration London

DAVID MITCHELL

> It's not to say what a Bankers Skill in this sense will honestly extend to: Il'e tell you they are archer Men in their Trade than you and I think of.[1]
>
> For the workemanshipp of such piece he shalbe by the viewe and judgement of the fowre wardens... & two skilful workemen ... adjudged and declared to be a perfecte and skillful workeman.[2]

This paper provides a context for the concerns to be addressed throughout this book. Firstly, it outlines the historiography of the goldsmiths' trade. Secondly, it discusses the concepts of innovation and skill. Thirdly, by reference to the development of the trade during the second half of the seventeenth century, it rehearses some of the outstanding problems and disputed questions that are to be considered.

Traditionally, London goldsmiths exercised diverse functions in the handling of precious metals: the manufacture and sale of plate and jewellery, the provision of certain financial services, the refining of gold and silver, and the exercise of specific roles in government finance and the Mint.[3] Some businesses were engaged concurrently in several of these activities, but the detailed structure of the trade is at present unresolved, especially in the seventeenth century. Early in the century, the range of financial services was largely confined to foreign exchange dealings and the provision of loans against the security of pawned plate or jewellery. A pamphlet, *The Mystery of the New Fashioned Goldsmiths or Bankers* published in 1676, described goldsmiths prior to the Civil War as of the 'Old fashion' and stated,

> their whole employment was to make and sell Plate, to buy forreign Coyns and Gold and Silver imported to melt and cull them, and cause some to be culled at the Mint, and with the rest to furnish the Refiners, Plate-makers, and Merchants, as they found the price of gold and silver to vary, and as Merchants had occasion for Forrein Coyns.[4]

The author bemoaned the rise of goldsmith-bankers but recognised the cardinal changes which, during the Commonwealth, had transformed the nature of the financial services that they provided; namely, the incidence of non-interest bearing credit accounts and the lending of 'not their own but other mens money'. The goldsmiths made a major contribution to the 'Financial Revolution' of the late seventeenth and early eighteenth

---

[1] *Is not the Hand of Joab in all this?* or *An Enquiry into the Grounds of a late pamphlet intituled The Mystery of the New Fashioned Goldsmiths or Bankers* (London, 1676), p. 13.
[2] Goldsmiths' Company, Court Book O, ff. 551–2, Regulations for masterpieces, 1607.
[3] Also the associated uses of precious metals in decorating textiles, furniture, arms and armour.
[4] J R, *The Mystery of the New Fashioned Goldsmiths or Bankers* (London, 1676), p. 3.

century, but its exact character remains unclear.[5] The Restoration was also a period of change in the design of plate and the organisation of its manufacture, in response to demands for items in the 'new' or 'French' fashion. London goldsmiths thus occupied a central position both in relation to crucial developments in the economy and in patterns of consumption which took place in England during that period. In the process, the structure of their own trade underwent fundamental change.

Historiography

The signal reason for the lack of a comprehensive understanding of the structure of the trade lies in its historiography, where there has been a great divide between financial history and the history of plate. The former was written by economic historians who concerned themselves with foreign exchange, the development of the banking system, the origin of the Bank of England, and the early histories of certain surviving banks.[6] In contrast, the history of plate was written initially by independent antiquaries, and subsequently by art historians, either from museums or auction houses. These studies, from the seminal work of Octavius Morgan, have been driven, shaped and classified according to 'makers marks'.[7] In this approach, the objects have been characterised primarily in relation to 'heroic creators', identified by their marks.

The study of marks developed out of an eighteenth-century interest in plate, reflected in several articles in *Archaeologia* and *The Gentleman's Magazine*.[8] Ten years after Morgan's pioneering study of 1853, William Chaffers published a handbook of hallmarks and, some twenty years later, a history of English goldsmiths and their marks, *Gilda Aurifabrorum*.[9] As Helen Clifford has observed, he recognised the problem of 'authorship':

> there are necessarily in every piece of decorative plate three parties to whom credit of production must be ascribed, viz. the artist who designs it, the plate worker who makes it, and the goldsmith who sells it and becomes the publisher. [10]

However, Chaffers seems to have largely ignored the complexities inherent in this understanding, as his work implies that the 'makers mark' belonged solely to the actual

---

[5] P.G.M. Dickson, *The Financial Revolution in England: A study in the Development of Public Credit, 1688–1756* (London, 1967); C. Clay, *Public Finance and Private Wealth: The Career of Sir Stephen Fox, 1627–1716* (Oxford, 1978); D.W. Jones, *War and Economy* (Oxford, 1988); E. Kerridge, *Trade and Banking in Early Modern England* (Manchester, 1988); L. Neal, *The Rise of Financial Capitalism* (Cambridge, 1990).

[6] B.E. Supple, *Commercial Crisis and Change in England 1600–1642* (Cambridge, 1959); R.D. Richards, 'The first fifty years of the Bank of England (1694–1744)', in J.G. van Dillen (ed.), *History of the Principal Public Banks* (The Hague, 1934); Sir John Clapham, *The Bank of England* (Cambridge, 1944); F.T. Melton, *Sir Robert Clayton and the Origins of English Deposit Banking 1658–1685* (Cambridge, 1986); F.G. Hilton Price, *Handbook of London Bankers* (London,1890–1).

[7] O. Morgan, 'On the assay marks on gold and silver plate', *Archaeological Journal*, 34 (London, 1853).

[8] J. Culme, 'Attitudes to Old Plate 1750–1900', *The Directory of Gold and Silversmiths, 1838–1914* (2 vols; Woodbridge, 1987), vol 1, pp. xvi–xxxvi.

[9] W. Chaffers, *Hallmarks on Gold and Silver Plate* (London, 1863); *Gilda Aurifabrorum, A History of English Goldsmiths and Plateworkers and their Marks Stamped on Plate* (London, 1883).

[10] Quoted in H. Clifford, 'Paul de Lamerie and the organisation of the London goldsmiths' trade in the first half of the eighteenth century', in S. Hare (ed.), *Paul de Lamerie* (London, 1990).

manufacturer, without further qualification. His attitudes were clearly influenced by Ruskin's idea of 'the Artist', for he quotes him at length:

> So long, observe, as fashion has influence on the manufacture of plate — so long you cannot have a goldsmith's art in this country. Do you suppose any workman, worthy of the name, will put his brains into a cup or a urn which he knows is to go to the melting-pot in half a score of years?
>
> ... true goldsmith's work, when it exists, is generally the means of education of the greatest painters and sculptors of the day ... Ghiberti was a goldsmith, and beat out the bronze gates which Michael Angelo said might serve for the gates of Paradise.[11]

In 1878, five years before *Gilda Aurifabrorum*, Cripps had published *Old English Plate*.[12] This opens with an account of the use of the 'worker's' or 'maker's' mark without any qualification of its significance, and follows with sections which describe plate by type: spoons, mazers and so on. Thus the die was cast for the 'object-centred approach' which 'has bedevilled silver studies in the past century.'[13] The study of hallmarks and the classification of plate by form and style continued in a similar vein, although some writers began to examine the relationships between style, the method of manufacture and the nature of materials. For example, Jackson thought that the use of Britannia silver after 1697 resulted in design changes:

> As soon as it became obvious to the plate workers of the time, that [Britannia silver] was not sufficient to give the hardness necessary to prevent work of a fine and delicate character from soon showing signs of wear, many of them ... preferred to express their art in designs having fewer ornamental lines, and those more strongly marked than had been usual in the preceding period.[14]

Before and after the Second World War, Oman and then Hayward, whilst continuing in this tradition, also investigated the sources of design and began to consider the way plate responded to changing customs in dining.[15] In addition, Hayward raised the question of how skill was transferred from foreign to native craftsmen:

> We find a small group of English-born makers who successfully adopted the grand manner of the Huguenots. Foremost among them are the brothers George and Francis Garthorne and Benjamin Pyne. Whether these goldsmiths employed Huguenot journeymen or did in fact master the new style themselves is a problem that we cannot at present solve.[16]

With hindsight, Arthur Grimwade's *Rococo Silver*, published in 1974, could be considered a watershed.[17] The book, the third in a series, was preceded by monographs on Caroline and Huguenot silver by Oman and Hayward, respectively. Although the work is of modest length, the author considered many of the topics that have remained of scholarly concern. These include: the development of style, the identification of

---

[11] Quoted in Chaffers, *Gilda Aurifabrorum*, p. 7.
[12] W.J. Cripps, *Old English Plate* (London, 1878).
[13] P. Glanville, *Silver in Tudor and Early Stuart England* (London, 1990), p. 11.
[14] C.J. Jackson, *An Illustrated History of English Plate* (2 vols; London, 1911) vol 1, p. 266. This view was repeated by E. Wenham, *Domestic Silver of Great Britain and Ireland* (Oxford, 1931), p. 21.
[15] C. Oman, *English Domestic Silver* (London, 1934); *English Silversmiths' Work Civil and Domestic* (London, 1965); *Caroline Silver, 1625–1688* (London, 1970); *English Engraved Silver* (London, 1978).
[16] J.F. Hayward, *Huguenot Silver in England, 1688-1727* (London, 1959), p. 8.
[17] A. Grimwade, *Rococo Silver* (London, 1974).

design sources, the structure of the trade, workshop practice, subcontracting and the growth of specialisation, the changing geography of goldsmiths' shops, and not least, the significance of the maker's mark.[18] Grimwade, together with Norman Penzer, had been instrumental in saving the Garrard Ledgers from pulping. These have since formed the basis of studies by Elaine Barr and Helen Clifford which give important new insights into the structure of the trade in the eighteenth century and the process of design, manufacture, and marketing.[19] Grimwade's concerns have all been taken further by Philippa Glanville, but with additional emphasis on the placing of silver wares within their economic, social and cultural context.[20]

Innovation and Skill

There are several dictionary definitions of 'innovation' which are appropriate to this discussion: 'the alteration of what is established by the introduction of new elements or forms', 'a change made in the nature or fashion of anything; something newly introduced; a novel practice or method'. During the sixteenth century, the word 'innovation' (used but rarely), was applied disapprovingly to changes in religious belief or practice: 'to traduce him as an author of suspitious innovation.' Even in the next century, when the word was applied more generally it still had negative connotations: 'The hydra-headed multitude that only gape for innovation.' It was only during the nineteenth century that innovation acquired respectability and was employed in the positive way that characterises its use within these pages. In the goldsmith's trade innovation took several forms: commercial innovations in the provision of financial services; the introduction of new forms and styles to the product range; and technical changes in the methods of manufacture.

The definitions of 'skill' that are germane to this discussion are: 'capability of accomplishing something with precision and certainty; practical knowledge in combination with ability; cleverness, expertness', and 'knowledge or understanding of something'. Although there were other uses of the word that are now archaic, these meanings of 'skill' were already current around 1600:

> But now is the people mightely increased bothe in number of people and in all good skill, and skilfull of alle kinde and manner of trades.[21]

The two quotations at the opening of this chapter indicate that skill was perceived in both the embodied knowledge of the banker and the manual dexterity of the silversmith. Nevertheless, even when usages of the word 'skill' appear to be identical, there are doubtless nuances of meaning in these quotations that are not apparent to the modern reader, as the concept of skill is, in a sense, 'socially constructed'. The public letter-writer in Kipling's *Kim* who composed Mahbub Ali's telegrams in the Kashmir Serai was respected for his skills in reading and writing, whereas these accomplishments were required as a matter of course for a goldsmith-banker's apprentice in Restoration London.

---

[18] The maker's mark was discussed in a number of other works including J. Banister, *English Silver* (London, 1965) p 37; H. Honour, *Goldsmiths & Silversmiths* (London, 1971), pp. 21–22.
[19] E. Barr, *George Wickes, Royal Goldsmith 1698–1761* (London, 1980); H. Clifford, 'Parker and Wakelin, the study of an eighteenth-century goldsmithing business, with particular reference to the Garrard Ledgers, 1760-1766', unpublished Ph.D. thesis, Royal College of Art, London, 1989.
[20] P. Glanville, *Silver in England* (London, 1987); *Silver in Tudor and Early Stuart England*.
[21] British Library, Lansdowne 152, f. 237: Petition of 13 July 1608.

Financial Services

It seems that the provision of credit accounts and the development of the clearing system took place around 1650 among goldsmiths in Lombard Street. As is described in Stephen Quinn's paper, this system, based upon the agreement of a ring of goldsmiths to accept each others 'notes', in effect to honour third-party debts, was the vital step in the establishment of goldsmith banking. Neither the conditions of those agreements nor the parties to them are known in any detail. At least two distinct groups emerged: one, centred in Lombard Street, apparently served City tradesmen and overseas merchants, while the other, in Fleet Street, had a different clientele of nobility, gentry and lawyers. Of the forty-four goldsmith-bankers or 'Goldsmiths that keep Running Cashes' recorded in 1677, twenty-nine were in Lombard Street and Cornhill, eleven in Fleet Street, the Strand and Covent Garden, and the remaining four in Cheapside.[22]

It was stated at the time, and since repeated, that credit accounts were non-interest bearing: 'the Goldsmiths sought to be the Merchants Cash-keepers to receive and pay for nothing'.[23] A preliminary examination of the papers of both Robert Blanchard and Thomas Fowle shows that this was the case among the Fleet Street group, but there are indications that those in Lombard Street paid interest on credit accounts.[24] A typical customer of the Lombard Street goldsmith-bankers was the merchant adventurer William Attwood who traded principally with Hamburg. He dealt with a dozen different goldsmith-bankers between 1655 and 1670 including Edward Backwell (Fig. 25, p. 56), the Viners, and the Meynells.[25] To some of them, Attwood sold rixdollars or negotiated bills of exchange. To others, particularly to Backwell, he lent money, occasionally borrowed it, and kept a credit account which he used to pay his bills and sometimes to purchase plate. A significant proportion of the money that Attwood lent Backwell was on behalf of his Hamburg partner George Watson. He received between 4 ½ per cent and 5 ½ per cent interest depending upon the year and the length of call upon the money. Attwood was keen to receive the best rate for in 1666 he reported to Watson:

> I did speak with Sir Robert Vynor, and told him I did expect he should allow me 6% (my Father [in-law] Pell was then by, to whom he allowed that rate. He said what he allowed others he would allow.[26]

The transactions detailed in Attwood's books are replicated in Backwell's ledgers where clearing accounts are also found with most of Attwood's other bankers.[27]

It is significant that Viner was willing, albeit under pressure, to pay 6 per cent on the money that he borrowed, as this was the maximum legal interest rate that could be charged. If he borrowed at 6 per cent he could not profitably lend the money to a third party at the same rate. One of the main complaints against the goldsmith-bankers, voiced by the

---

[22] Samuel Lee, *The Little London Directory* (London, 1677).
[23] J R, *New Fashioned Goldsmiths*, p. 3.
[24] D.M. Mitchell, '"Mr Fowle, Pray pay the washwoman": the trade of a London goldsmith-banker, 1660–1692', *Business and Economic History*, 23, no. 1 (Williamsburg, Virginia, Fall 1994), pp. 27–38.
[25] Public Record Office (PRO), C109/19 to 24. Goldsmith-bankers include: Backwell, Thomas and Robert Viner, Edmond and Benjamin Hinton, John Colvill, George Day, Jeremiah Snow, Francis and Isaac Meynell, Francis Jeyne.
[26] PRO, C109/23 Part II, Copybook of Correspondence, Letter of 1 June 1666.
[27] Royal Bank of Scotland Archives, London, Backwell Ledgers, EB 1/1 to 4.

writer of a pamphlet in 1676 was that they charged 'by private contracts', 10, 20, or even 30 per cent interest, and indeed that they needed at least 9 per cent to run their businesses.[28] In the same year, a pamphlet refuting those claims appeared.[29] The author described instances where 10 per cent could be made quite legally and concluded with the point that the goldsmith-bankers were cheaper than the scriveners, who charged at least 12 per cent. By their nature these 'private' or parole contracts are not prominent among Bankers' papers, although Thomas Fowle's pocket-book lists gratuities which were probably lump sum payments representing the difference between the rate of interest formally specified in the loan bond or note, and the rate which was actually charged under a verbal agreement.[30]

Fig. 1. The Exchequer Office where specie was deposited by the goldsmith-bankers was probably similar to this supposed view of the Bank of England c.1695
(Bank of England)

There seems to have been little contact between the two main groups of goldsmith-bankers, in Lombard Street and in the vicinity of Fleet Street, respectively, although there may have been clearing arrangements between them. Two events perhaps gave the Fleet Street group a competitive advantage, at least for a while. The Great Fire stopped short of Temple Bar but destroyed Lombard Street. Six years later, the 'stop' on the Exchequer in 1672 was a setback to several of the Lombard Street goldsmiths, whilst only Mawson of those in Fleet Street was large enough to have lent significant sums to the Crown. Nevertheless, the memory of the stop may have coloured the goldsmith-bankers' reaction in 1689, when huge sums were required to finance the war. Bankers like Sir Francis Child seemed only willing to lend that proportion of their funds that did not leave them dangerously exposed to default by the Crown (Fig. 1).[31]

[28] J R, *New Fashioned Goldsmiths,* pp. 5–7.
[29] *Is not the Hand of Joab in all this?*
[30] PRO, C104/120 part I, Brown leather pocket-book.
[31] S. Quinn, 'Tallies or Reserves? Sir Francis Child's balance between capital reserves and extending credit to the Crown, 1685–1695', *Business and Economic History,* 23 (Williamsburg, Virginia, 1994), pp. 39–51.

The imperatives that led by about 1730 to the demise of the goldsmith-banker, whose principal functions came to be divided between the specialist bankers and large retailers, remain to be explored. In the case of the Lombard Street goldsmith Edward Backwell, it seems that the Great Fire, which destroyed his premises, was the catalyst that caused him to specialise in banking at the expense of selling plate and jewellery, but the extent to which his decision reflects a broader trend is not known. Some goldsmiths were involved in the international bullion market.[32] Others dealt extensively in diamonds, but it is unclear whether this was primarily for making jewellery or whether it represented a wholesale, speculative trade.[33] Relations between the goldsmith-bankers and other emergent groups are also uncertain: these include the scrivener-bankers, and the Sephardic merchants involved in the bullion and diamond trades.

Consumption of Plate

In contrast to their provision of financial services, the goldsmiths' trade in plate was marginal to London's overall economic growth. Yet the period was marked by a shift from importing to exporting silverwares, a clear sign of the growing appreciation of the quality and style of London-made plate and of the skill of its goldsmiths. Around 1600, there had been imports of plate, particularly from Nuremberg, and in the middle of the century, to judge from complaints, smallwares (buckles, buttons, bodkins, etc) were imported in some quantity.[34] Thereafter imports were few, including direct aristocratic purchases of French plate. In the late seventeenth century there were some exports to the American colonies and in the eighteenth century, after the restrictions on the export of plate had been relaxed, increased quantities were sent both to the colonies and to several European countries.[35] Recorded exports were on a modest scale — less than 5 per cent by weight of the plate touched at Goldsmiths' Hall, according to the Inspector-General's Ledgers — but it is clear that some substantial consignments to the royal houses of Russia and Portugal evaded the official record.[36] It has been suggested that both the forms and styles of some of these exported London wares influenced goldsmiths in Scandinavia and elsewhere. There has been little investigation of the overall quantity of plate produced. Records of the plate touched at Goldsmiths' Hall show that there had been a dramatic growth during the first forty years of the seventeenth century, but that production was brought almost to a halt by the Civil War (Fig. 2). The recovery which began in 1648 was set back by the Plague in 1665 and the Great Fire the following year, but by the 1670s production had returned to the level of the 1630s. For the next fifty years, apart from the crisis of the coinage which resulted in the introduction of the Britannia Standard in 1697, production

---

[32] S. Quinn, 'Banking before the Bank: London's unregulated goldsmith-bankers, 1660–1694' (unpublished Ph.D. thesis, University of Illinois 1994), pp. 190–210. Bullion Book of Stephen Evance.

[33] Both Thomas Fowle and his nephew Robert Fowle were members of diamond importing consortia, which also included English noblemen, English and Sephardic merchants (PRO C104/108). For Child's diamond trade see E.R Samuel, 'Sir Francis Child's jewellery business', *Three Banks Review* (March 1977).

[34] Glanville, *Silver in Tudor and Early Stuart England*, chapter 5, 'The Market for Imported Plate'.

[35] M. Gandy Fales, *Early American Silver* (New York, 1973), p. 4.

[36] Hayward, *Huguenot Silver*, p. 11.

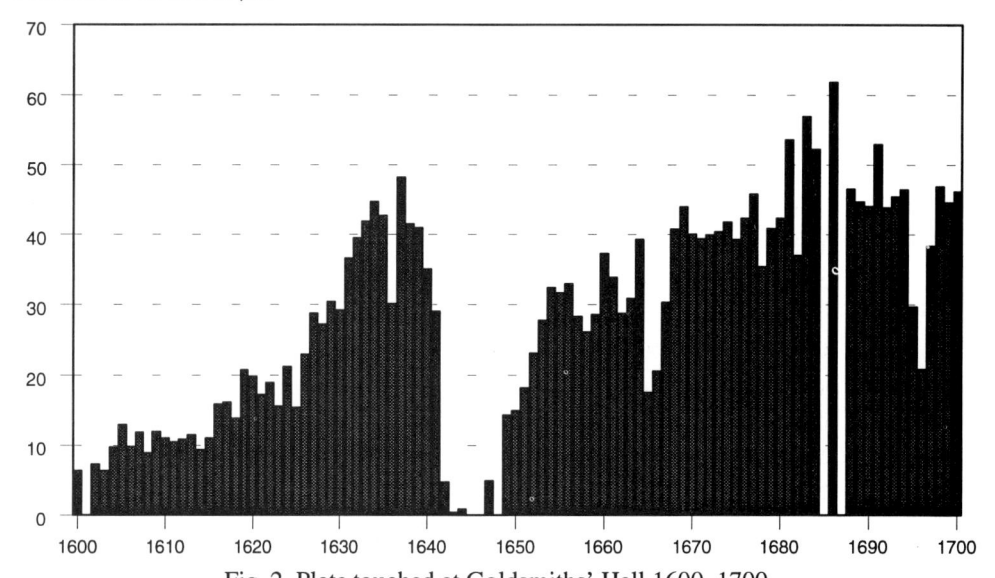

Fig. 2. Plate touched at Goldsmiths' Hall 1600–1700
Source: Goldsmiths' Company Court Books O to Z, and 1 to 10

fluctuated between that level and an increase of about a quarter.[37] If the assumption is correct that the quantities touched bore a nearly constant relation to total production, then this increase of a quarter is modest by comparison with London's growth in wealth and population. This needs to be reconciled with the judgements of the recent body of writing on the increase in consumption over the period.[38]

There are several possible explanations of the phenomenon. Firstly, that increased opportunities for investment in a variety of easily-redeemable financial instruments, coupled with changing fashions in dining and the display of buffet plate reduced the proportion of individual movable wealth invested in plate. Secondly, that a wider ownership of plate was linked to an enlarged secondhand market, which restricted the melting down and re-fashioning of old plate. Thirdly, certain drinking vessels and plates were increasingly made of glass and delftware rather than of silver. Lastly, that changes in demand for plate of particular types and form resulted in an increase in the number of pieces made for a given weight of plate touched, as they were of a lighter average weight.

Demand and Product Innovation

Although Chaffers recognised a collective authorship when he gave credit to the artist, the plate worker and the goldsmith, he omitted to assign any role to the purchaser. For

---

[37] Not all new plate, but only that to be offered for sale had to be touched. However, there is no present reason to believe that the proportion of total production that was touched varied considerably over this period, i.e. the quantity touched is here assumed to be a constant percentage of total production.

[38] N. McKendrick, J. Brewer and J.H. Plumb, *The Birth of a Consumer Society* (London, 1982); L. Weatherill, *Consumer Behaviour and Matenal Culture in Britain 1660–1760* (London, 1988); P. Earle, *The Making of the English Middle Class* (London, 1989); C. Shammas, *The Pre-industrial Consumer in England and America* (Oxford, 1990); J. Styles, 'Manufacturing, consumption and design in eighteenth-century England' in J. Brewer and R. Porter (eds.), *Consumption and the World of Goods* (London, 1993).

plate made to commission, the purchaser presumably played a part in specifying the piece, in terms of its size, weight, form or style, and possibly also influenced the design. Chaffer's model describes a nineteenth-century scenario, with a specialist retailer commissioning the design, organising and financing its manufacture and putting it in his window for general sale. Apart from the employment of an 'artist' or specialist designer, which appears to have been rare in the seventeenth century, the model is but one of several possible patterns of production for the earlier period. It is necessary to assess, within those several patterns, which individuals exercised the initiative for specification, design and the organisation of manufacture, and to determine the degree to which one person orchestrated the whole process.

One such pattern of production in Restoration London was centred on the goldsmith-banker, who organised a network of subcontractors and specialist makers to satisfy the call for new forms and styles of plate. Some of these demands reflected changes in social behaviour. The new practice among noblewomen of entertaining formally in their private apartments led to a demand for splendid dressing plate (see front cover). Others stemmed from the introduction of new beverages, which required services for tea, coffee and chocolate. Other product innovations included sconces and branch candlesticks, pepper and mustard pots, and fruit dishes.[39] Existing wares such as salts were made in new square forms (Fig. 3) and candlesticks both square and octagonal. Many of these expensive wares were made in the 'New' or 'French Fashion': terms which were often used in both Backwell's and Blanchard's ledgers to describe candlesticks, sugar bowls, spoons and forks, and occasionally other items such as salts, porringers, cups, basons and ewers.[40] Although these objects might be described today as in the 'international style', the contemporary perception was that they were in the French style. This possibly says more about English acceptance of the cultural suzerainty of France rather than the particular styles current at the time in Paris.

Fig. 3. The Moody Salt, mark of Wolfgang Howzer, London 1664/5.
(Victoria and Albert Museum)

The leading goldsmith-bankers were among those active in meeting these demands. They may have accounted for a significant proportion of the plate sold in the metropolis and for the majority of the new fashioned wares. In 1662/3 Sir Robert Viner provided 44,100 oz to the Crown alone and in just nine months of 1663 Edward Backwell sold 16,000 oz (Table 1). Despite being the 'father of English banking', Backwell in 1663 sold

---

[39] Fruit dishes, i.e. chased footed salvers of the type given by the Earl of Carlisle to the Tzar; see J. Culme (ed.), *English Silver Treasures from the Kremlin* (London, 1991), No. 106.
[40] Royal Bank of Scotland Archives, Backwell, I and Child, CH/194/1 and 2.

TABLE 1
Plate Sales (in ounces)

	1663	1664	1665	1666	1667
Sir Robert VYNOR[1]	44,100				
Edward BACKWELL[2]	21,300				
Robert BLANCHARD[3]	3,900	3,600	1,000	2,500	1,400
Thomas FOWLE[4]	-	1,500	1,000	4,000	
Total quantitites touched at Hall[5]	370,000	471,600	209,700	246,000	363,600

[1] Jewel House Warrants, PRO LC5/107, 14 February 1662/3, sales to the Crown only.
[2] Royal Bank of Scotland Archives, Backwell's ledger I, April to December 1663, 16,000 oz in 9 months, i.e. pro rata 21,300 oz for one year.
[3] Royal Bank of Scotland Archives, Child's ledgers, CH/194/1 & 2, totals for January to December in each year. Shop was closed between 15 July 1665 and 9 January 1665/6 during the Plague.
[4] '1664 Daybook', PRO C114/179, periods are July 1664 to July 1665, closed between 17 July 1665 and 15 January 1665/6 during the Plague; then 15 January 1665/6 to 27 August 1666 (7.5 months), closed between 2 and 17 September owing to the Great Fire; finally 17 September 1666 to 9 September 1667.
[5] Goldsmiths' Company Court Books 4 and 5, totals are for approximately a year from June or July in each year, i.e. the entry for 1663 is from the summer of 1662.

plate and jewellery to over 200 customers. About three-quarters of them were City merchants and tradesmen, and less than a quarter peers, knights and esquires. Just thirteen were women, of whom six were peeresses. About 70 per cent of the plate by weight was in the form of plain wares; trenchers, plates, cups, basins and ewers sold at between 5s. 6d. and 5s. 8d./oz. Less than 10 per cent was of the 'new fashion' which was mostly sold to aristocratic customers at between 6s. 4d. and 8s./oz: for example, chased salvers and dressing plate to the Earl and Countess of Carlisle, two gilt cups to the Queen Mother and a pair of gilt and crystal candlesticks to Lady Bruce. After the Great Fire, Backwell ceased retailing plate and jewellery and just executed commissions for a few powerful clients. Thus it is possible in 1666/7 to identify particular objects with specific fashioning changes. In that year, Wolfgang Howzer made several items, including six salvers for Lady Fanshaw and two wall candlesticks for the Duke of York, for which he was paid at the rate of 10d./oz.[41] In 1663, Howzer had been paid £48 for fashion which suggests that he supplied about 1150 oz of plate, or most of the new fashioned plate that Backwell sold at that time. In contrast, the fashioning cost of plain wares such as trencher plates was 4d./oz.[42]

Robert Blanchard's business at Temple Bar, Fleet Street, was very different in scale from Backwell's in Lombard Street. It had been established before the Civil War under William Wheeler and by 1663 was a medium size operation, selling plate and jewellery to seventy customers as well as providing credit accounts and various types of loans. The client profile was very different from Backwell's, reflecting their respective locations.

[41] Royal Bank of Scotland Archives, Backwell, P, f. 234v. Wolfgang Howzer account: Paid £25 for fashioning 611 oz 15 dwt of plate or 9.8d./oz. Plate consisted of: 6 salvers and warming pan cover, 328 oz 8 dwt sold to Lady Fanshaw @ 6s. 6d./oz; 2 gilded scabbards, 10 oz 13 dwt sold to the Treasury @ 7s./oz plus 2s./oz for gilding; 2 wall candlesticks, 283 oz sold to the Duke of York @ 9s./oz (presumably also gilded).
[42] Backwell, P, f. 218, 25 Jan 1666/7. Thomas Starkey was paid £6. 17s. 6d. for fashioning 24 trencher plates; 413 oz 10 dwt or 4d./oz. The plates were sold to Lady Fanshaw on 16 Feb 1666/7 @ 5s. 7d./oz. Backwell O, f. 634v, 3 Aug 1666 Francis Leeke was paid 19s. for fashioning 4 stands, 57 oz @ 4d./oz. Plain wares also made by Abraham Cheare, William Harrison, John Innis, Mr [Jacob?] Harris and Mr Hughes.

Half of Blanchard's sales were to peers, knights, esquires or their wives and almost a third of the total sales were to women. As might be expected, a much higher percentage of Blanchard's sales were of new fashioned plate.[43] Thomas Fowle's shop was also at Temple Bar, but when his 'Daybook' opens in 1664, his trade was in its infancy. It was only after the Great Fire that he started to supply new fashioned wares which were made by Wolfgang Howzer, Jacob Bodendick (Fig. 4) and Arthur Manwaring.[44]

Backwell's, Blanchard's and Fowle's accounts all demonstrate the great advantage of the credit account to the goldsmith in his role of retailer, for payment for plate was made by a simple transfer from credit to debit. This avoided the extensive and extended debts owed by purchasers which were such a feature of life for most retailers in the luxury trades at this period, whether they were selling silks, watches or coaches.

Plate manufacture

There are several important questions concerning the organisation of the manufacturing process, particularly the degree of specialisation, and the nature of subcontractors and specialist suppliers. There were specialist spoonmakers in London during the sixteenth century, and in 1607 the Goldsmiths' Company complained that some goldsmiths were willing to be simply 'hammermen'.[45] Apparently, such complaints had little effect, for by 1720 specialisation was a highly-developed feature of the trade. Nonetheless, it is unclear whether certain practices, known for the later eighteenth century, were already established. These included the habit among retailers of stamping their mark on the wares of subcontractors, some of whom were substantial silversmiths who never registered a mark of their own.[46] In the 1670s the Company and others asserted that certain English silversmiths marked pieces that were either chased or wholly made by stranger silversmiths, employed, against the Company's regulations, as journeymen or subcontractors.[47] These assertions, coupled with the quality of post-Restoration 'new fashioned' plate, have led

Fig. 4. Candlestick in the 'new' fashion. Mark of Jacob Bodendick, London c. 1665 (27 oz 10 dwt plus 3 oz socket.)
(Victoria and Albert Museum)

---

[43] Royal Bank of Scotland Archives, Child, CH/194/1 and 2.
[44] Mitchell, "Mr Fowle"; and D.M. Mitchell, 'Dressing Plate by the unknown London silversmith "W"', *The Burlington Magazine* (London, June 1973).
[45] T. Kent, *London Silverspoonmakers* (London, 1981). Goldsmiths' Company, Court Book O ff. 1551–2, 4 Nov 1607 Masterpieces.
[46] Clifford, 'Parker and Wakelin'.
[47] Goldsmiths' Company, Court Books: 4 f. 42, Candlesticks marked by John Hill but made by a Dutch man 'who wrought with him as a journeyman; 6 f. 1 various wares with Robert Alvey's mark made by one 'Welch a dutchman' who was supplied with the silver by Alvey'; 7 f.193v. Arthur Manwaring and Jacob Harris were accused of marking aliens' plate.

to the suspicion that much of it was made by strangers, but it is far from certain that this was in fact the case.

The subcontractors used by Viner and Blanchard are largely unknown, although from Sir Robert's Commission of Bankruptcy in 1684, it appears that the New Year's gifts that he supplied in 1671 were made by Francis Leeke [Leake] and Richard Marchant, with some of them gilded by Charles Round.[48] There is considerably more information for the network of subcontractors and suppliers used by Edward Backwell and Thomas Fowle. Certain operations such as gilding and engraving were carried out by specialists. Fowle used the gilder Charles Round and the engraver Mr Trevelyan whilst Backwell paid both Mr Collet and Peter White for engraving. Planishing and burnishing were the province of women, generally the wives or widows of silversmiths, such as Mrs Horne, the burnisher employed by Fowle, and Mrs Adderton and Mrs Innis by Backwell. Women also made smallwares and some jewellery: Fowle paid Mrs Horne for fashioning buckles and clasps, Mrs Greene for thimbles, Mrs Winter and 'the Frenchwoman' for rings.[49] Apart from Mr Greene and Mr Winter, who also worked for Fowle, John Innis was paid over several years by Backwell for mending old and making new plate. Innis together with Francis Leeke and Thomas Starkey were former apprentices of Henry Starkey. All four silversmiths were employed as subcontractors by Backwell, who also commissioned the plateworkers William Harrison and Abraham Cheare — both pupils of Abraham Smith. Clearly in discharging large orders, such as that for Prince Rupert in 1670 which weighed 3,270 oz in total, Backwell found it an advantage to employ a group of subcontractors and specialist makers who knew each other well and could co-operate to produce wares in similar styles, to the required deadline.[50]

Backwell commissioned mourning rings by the hundred from several jewellers including William Lovett, Robert Welsted, Mr Sharp and Mr Thursby; he used the Frenchman Isaac Mobart for cutting diamonds and 'his freind' Mr Caillate for cutting rubies. Specialist subcontractors were also used for particular types of plate including flatware, casters, chafing dishes and snuffers. Fowle used John King for flatware and Marlyn Gale for casters and chafing dishes. It seems that Gale, like Howzer and presumably most subcontractors, worked concurrently for several goldsmiths, as he also supplied goods to Robert Blanchard and others.[51] Nevertheless, a few goldsmith-bankers may have had sufficient demand for particular types of goods to be able to monopolise a subcontractor's workshop. Thomas Fowle's trade continued to grow from the beginnings reflected in the '1664 Daybook'; by the late 1670s, he had become one of the leading

---

[48] PRO, C107/112 ff. 1–2.
[49] Mrs Horne was possibly Sara Horne of the Strand who was called before the Goldsmiths' Company in 1655 and again in 1661 for a substandard ring, bodkins, thimbles and buttons: Court Books I f.143 and 3 f. 125v. Mrs Greene was probably Elizabeth Greene, widow, of Foster Lane, the subject of a complaint to the Company from Thomas Fowle in 1683 for a substandard bodkin and thimble: Court Book 9 f. 64.
[50] Royal Bank of Scotland Archives, Backwell, S f. 108.
[51] Gale was in trouble with the Company on several occasions. He was free of the Carpenters' Company and in 1661 was accused of making substandard spoons for Mr Knight in Cheapside. He was fined and sworn a goldsmith: Court Book 3 f.136. In 1674, Blanchard complained of a substandard mustard pot and spoons and as he 'could not tell what damage he might formerly done unto him having byn by him imployed for divers yeares last past desired to have Mr Gales bond': Court Book 7 f.44v. Between 1664 and 1667, Gale supplied Fowle with sugar casters, mustard pots, chafing dishes and 'a handle candle stick: PRO C114/179.

Fig. 5. Powder box from the Calverley toilet service with plaquette
of Silenus. Mark of William Fowle, London 1683/4 (19 oz).
(Victoria and Albert Museum)

goldsmith-bankers in London. In 1681 his nephew William Fowle, on completion of his apprenticeship with Arthur Manwaring, was established by Thomas in a house and workshop off the Strand. Until his death just three years later, William fashioned, exclusively for his uncle, the most splendid chased and cast toilet services, (Fig. 5).[52]

Transfer of Information

For the seventeenth century, little is known of how instructions were passed between client, retailer and subcontractors. Some use was made of drawings, engraved designs, models, moulds, patterns, letters and verbal instructions, but the normal procedures and methods have yet to be established. Outline specifications from clients were presumably given verbally or by letter. Sir Richard Verney wrote to Thomas Fowle from Compton on 12 March 1684/5:

> I would have two Silver Badges for two musiteons [musicians] that I Give leveryes [liveries] too. I would not have them too Big by no means with either my Crest & Coate of arms I would have them sent downe by our Carrior next thursday if possible.

The livery badges were dispatched in haste as desired but were unsatisfactory as Verney wrote again on 2 April:

---

[52] Mitchell, 'Dressing Plate by "WF"'.

> Mr Fowle, those Badges are not Right so that I would have them Altred. The Crest and the Verneys Coate in the selfe same way as the other was don [a sketch of the arms is drawn in the middle of the letter] Raised and two silvre chaines to wear with them.[53]

In 1696 there is correspondence between Robert Fowle, Thomas's nephew, and Lord Ossulton about livery badges and buttons for the seven watermen to man his new barge. They were very expensive, with the badges costing 8s. 10d./oz. These were presumably cast from a specially designed mould, but unfortunately the correspondence does not indicate whether it was shown to Ossulton for his approval before the badges were made.[54] Moulds and patterns may have been made by the commissioned silversmith or by a third party. The silver patterns used by William Fowle to cast the mythological plaquettes that he set into his toilet boxes and mirrors seem to have been made by another silversmith, probably by a stranger working at that time in London.[55]

The use of books of designs such as those by Christian van Vianen, Polifilio Zancarli and Simon Gribelin has been discussed by Oman, Lightbown and Hayward.[56] Oman also considered C.C. Dauterman's study of the flat-chased chinoiserie designs which were a notable feature of much plate bearing a variety of London sponsors' marks from the 1680s.[57] Dauterman thought that most of these wares were chased in a single shop. One of those who have challenged this interpretation is Philippa Glanville, who rejects the idea of a single specialist workshop. As the chinoiseries were chased by many different hands, she argues that the common thread lay with the 'pattern drawers', who produced designs on paper for the chasers to 'work up'. Not much is known of pattern drawers in London, but there were nine recorded in a survey of the 1692 poll tax returns. They were widely dispersed throughout the City and several were prosperous: William Murford and Nathaniel Hallhead in Cornhill ward both kept three men and one woman servant, and were assessed for stocks of £100 and rack rents of £60 and £40 respectively; Thomas Astley in Faringdon Within was also assessed for £100 of stocks and although he kept no journeymen, he had two apprentices.[58] Unfortunately, it is not known if these men produced patterns for goldsmiths, for there were other craftsmen that may have used their skill, particularly linen and cotton printers, silk weavers and perhaps delftware potters.

If the assumption is correct that the early modern elite craftsman had a considerable capacity to draw, then designs and instructions may have been transmitted by sketches. Their preparation would have been facilitated by the considerable increase in the volume of printed material in the second half of the seventeenth century, not only of engraved designs but also illustrated books, trade cards and broadsheets.

It is possible that the geographical disposition of the parties reflected the methods used to transfer information. For example, if verbal instructions were regularly given

---

[53] PRO C104/107.
[54] PRO C104/123 doc 138 and C104/120 Part I doc. 245.
[55] Mitchell, 'Dressing Plate by "WF"'.
[56] Oman, *Caroline Silver*, pp. 14–23; R. Lightbown, 'Charles I and the art of the goldsmiths', in A. MacGregor (ed.) *The Late King's Goods* (London, 1989), pp. 233–255; Hayward, *Huguenot Silver*, pp. 66–75.
[57] C.C. Dauterman, 'Dream pictures of Cathay: chinoiserie on Restoration silver', *Bulletin of the Metropolitan Museum of Art* (New York, Summer 1964), pp. 11–25.
[58] Centre for Metropolitan History, 'Metropolitan London in the 1690s' project database.

by the retailer to the principal silversmith subcontractor, then close proximity would be required. Accordingly, it could be expected that after the Great Fire of 1666, some silversmiths would relocate from their traditional area around the Hall to the vicinity of Fleet Street, which was becoming a major retail centre for plate and jewellery. It is possible that Thomas Jenkins, who moved to Essex Street, and several of Thomas Fowle's subcontractors, who lived near Temple Bar, were part of such a general trend.[59] Arthur Grimwade has shown that in the middle of the eighteenth century, clusters of craftsmen were dispersed throughout the metropolis with only a rump remaining about the Hall.[60]

Technical and Stylistic Change

Technical and stylistic change was a feature of the trade after the Restoration. It has been generally accepted that immigrant or 'stranger' goldsmiths were influential both technically and in terms of the form and style of wares, although the degree of their influence has been questioned. Both before and after the Civil War, Christian van Vianen had a workshop in London. He was from a celebrated family of Utrecht goldsmiths, the son of Adam and nephew of Paulus van Vianen, whose auricular style he introduced into England.[61] From about 1660, there were a number of other economic immigrants, indifferently called 'Dutch' in English documents, although some were German or Swiss.[62] In 1676, a petition listed twenty-six stranger goldsmiths working in and about the City; two of them had sizeable workshops, John Cooqus, Christian van Vianen's son-in-law in Pall Mall, and John Cassan in Drury Lane.[63]

The period from the middle of the century until the arrival of significant numbers of Huguenot silversmiths, after the repeal of the edict of Nantes in 1685, is marked by fine chasing and applied work. Also, there was an apparent increased use of casting, although the full extent of this is not clear since there is no general agreement as to which pieces or parts of pieces have been chased and which cast. Similarly, there have been few systematic studies of serial production, either for the making of cast handles and knobs, or the use of stamping for spoons, buckles and buttons. Because of the lack of basic data, it is difficult to assess the merits of possible explanations of these developments: for example, whether the increased use of casting was to reduce unit costs by repetition, or was an attempt to maintain the quality of the product in view of the limited numbers of skilled chasers. There was also a greater use of complicated cut-card work which, like the tankards sheathed with embossed panels marked by Bodendick, required double-running solder techniques.

Many of these innovations, together with fashionable 'international' style chasing, seem to have been introduced by stranger goldsmiths; moreover much of the 'new fashioned' plate was made by men like Cooqus, Cassan, Howzer and Bodendick. Some fine quality chased and cast work, marked by English goldsmiths, was also clearly

---

[59] A. Grimwade and J. Banister, 'Thomas Jenkins unveiled', *Connoisseur* (July 1977).
[60] Grimwade, *Rococo Silver*, pp. 13–14.
[61] J.R. ter Molen, *Van Vianen* (Rotterdam, 1984).
[62] e.g. Wolfgang Howzer (Hauser) from Zürich and Jacob Bodendick from Limburg.
[63] Goldsmiths' Company, Court Book 7 f. 194v. Cooqus had five servants and Cassan three.

made by strangers although it seems that there were some Englishmen capable of making such pieces, for example, Arthur Manwaring and William Fowle.[64]

The Goldsmiths' Company

The Company largely confined itself to the regulation of apprenticeship and company membership, and the quality control of plate production. In effect this meant checking that the alloy used was of the correct standard, as little interest was taken in the quality of workmanship. This control was implemented through the Assay Office, which the Company operated on behalf of the Crown, and through the Company 'searches'. These were regularly made in London and occasionally in provincial cities.

At a time when the financial services provided by the goldsmith-bankers were growing both in number and importance, it is striking that the Company did not attempt to exercise any control over such matters, confining itself to its traditional roles. This raises the question as to why busy bankers concerned themselves with the affairs of the Company, often serving as Wardens and Assistants. Stephen Quinn argues that apprenticeship within the Company and opportunities for social exchange at the Hall provided the knowledge of an individual's competence, probity and financial soundness, a necessary prerequisite for the clearing system to operate effectively. A further reason for the close participation of goldsmith-bankers in the affairs of the Company may be that several of them accumulated the capital, upon which their banking business was initially based, through their trade in plate and jewellery. Thus they would have been interested in mundane matters such as the just and efficient organisation of the Assay Office and the regular searches. Moreover, as members of the Court, they could discreetly resist the repeated attempts of English silversmiths to prevent the 'strangers', upon whom the more substantial goldsmiths in part relied for the production of new fashioned wares, from working in London.

Most commentators have agreed that the 'strangers' were resented by native goldsmiths and by the Company. It has been observed that they often lived 'outside the City's jurisdiction', especially to the west, in St Martins in the Fields and Westminster, and were protected by royal and aristocratic patronage. The Company's action, or inaction, in relation to the strangers varied at different times, possibly as a result of such protection. However, if Backwell's and Fowle's employment of Howzer was typical, then the Company's position may have reflected the relative power of the vested interests of the goldsmith-bankers or the English workmen.

Training and the Transfer of Skill

Training for the trade was traditionally by apprenticeship. Christopher Challis has shown that the number of apprentices bound annually between 1630 and 1700 averaged about ninety but with only just over a third completing their terms and taking their freedom.[65] He suggested that the apparent high failure rate was misleading as a significant proportion of parents probably never intended their sons to take their

---

[64] Mitchell, 'Dressing Plate by "WF"'.
[65] C. Challis, 'Training and workshop practice in England in the seventeenth century', unpublished paper given at CMH/V&A/RCA Study Day, London, November 1993.

freedom, but regarded apprenticeship as a useful training and introduction to the world of affairs. Although the number of apprentices bound did not change significantly, except for the Civil War period, the length of their terms of indenture reduced steadily: in 1630-5, 13 per cent of apprentices were bound for seven years, 61 per cent for eight years, 21 per cent for nine years and 5 per cent for ten years; by 1690–5, the situation had changed dramatically with 92 per cent bound for seven years and the remaining 8 per cent for eight years. Several possible explanations have been advanced to explain this change. One is that as employment prospects improved, the parents of potential apprentices were able to negotiate shorter terms in return for higher premiums. A second, identified by Earle and others, is that with the growth of writing and mathematical schools, boys increasingly underwent one or two years of 'further' education before starting their apprenticeships at about the age of sixteen.[66]

Although some apprentices may have been sent to drawing masters, they learnt essentially by 'seeing and doing'. Skill was transferred within the workshop directly from master or journeyman to the apprentice. It is more difficult to understand the processes of skill transfer between stranger and native goldsmiths. The strangers' main influence may simply have been through the availability of their wares on the London market, and the consequent necessity for the natives to compete in quality, if not necessarily in form or style. There are some suggestions of more direct influence. Certain retailers, for example, employed stranger and English craftsmen simultaneously. Sometimes this was to make different types of wares, thus little contact need have been involved. In other cases, they made similar products, some of which may have required co-operation between the native and stranger craftsmen.[67] In a few cases, English boys are known to have been apprenticed to stranger silversmiths, while strangers also worked illegally as journeymen for English silversmiths.[68]

Philippa Glanville has pointed to two major differences between the training of English and continental apprentices: the *Wanderjahre* and the masterpiece.[69] English apprentices rarely travelled abroad, but it was customary in certain cities, particularly in the German-speaking lands, for silversmiths, after their initial years of training, to travel to one or more foreign centres to widen their experience. Among the young men who came to London during their *Wanderjahre* was Wolfgang Howzer (Hauser) who possibly also worked in Middelburg en route from Zurich.[70] His elder brother Hans Jacob was with him in London but returned home in 1663. Wolfgang stayed in England and his nephew Hans Heinrich, who had been apprenticed to his father Hans Jacob in 1675, joined him in London in 1681 during his own *Wanderjahre*.[71] The making and examination of a masterpiece was also required before many continental apprentices could become masters. In theory, the provision existed in London, but was very spasmodically enforced. There were detailed

---

[66] Earle, *English Middle Class*, chapter 3.
[67] Mitchell, 'Dressing Plate by "WF"'.
[68] e.g. Benjamin Pyne was apprenticed to the stranger George Bowers, who had a further five English apprentices. Jacob Bodendick had one English apprentice, Nathaniel Greene.
[69] Glanville, *Silver in Tudor and Early Stuart England*, pp. 86–88.
[70] J.H. Hessels (ed.) *Attestations or Certificates of Membership, Dutch Reformed Church, Austin Friars, 1528–1872* (London, 1892) No. 938, 14 April 1657, Certificate from Pieter Duvelaer, Minister at Middelburg.
[71] E.-M. Lösel, *Zürcher Goldschmiede Kunst* (Zürich, 1983), pp. 210–212.

Goldsmiths' Company regulations promulgated in 1607, but by 1640 the practice had fallen into disuse as the jewellers proposed:

> That noe Apprentize after he shall have served the space of seaven yeares or more shall presume to work or sett up for himselfe before hee shall make his Master peece or proof peece according to the custome of France Germany Italy and other Cuntreys. And as wee doe conceave hath ben the former Custome of this Company.[72]

Again in 1676, during the furore against stranger goldsmiths there was another attempt to insist that apprentices make a master piece before admittance to the freedom of the Company.[73]

Conventional conclusions are inappropriate in a paper such as this, that is primarily concerned with defining the outstanding problems and drawing attention, in the light of historiography, to the shortcomings of some of the solutions that have been previously suggested. However, the themes and questions which have emerged as significant in this discussion of the trade in Restoration London are relevant to the succeeding papers. Further research on the goldsmiths' trade is needed if there is to be a deeper understanding of its structure. This, together with similar studies on other luxury trades, could then reveal both the features which were unique to the goldsmiths' trade and those which were common to all.

---

[72] Goldsmiths' Company, Court Book J, V. 12, miscellaneous papers.
[73] Goldsmiths' Company, Court Book 7, f. 193.

Goldsmiths' apprenticeship during the first half of the seventeenth century: the situation in Paris

MICHÈLE BIMBENET-PRIVAT*

The basic training for Parisian goldsmiths, the guarantee of the quality of work and of the profession's reputation, was laid down in many regulations, of which the first were the statutes of the guild in 1355. From 1584, only craftsmen who had completed their apprenticeship in a Parisian workshop could become master goldsmiths in Paris, and thus during the seventeenth century apprenticeship was a vital stage in the career of a goldsmith.

It is interesting to study the regulations in force at the beginning of the seventeenth century to see how apprenticeships differed greatly in practice from what was prescribed in the statutes. Detailed information about the apprentices can be found in their contracts and from the records of disputes brought before the *Cour des Monnaies de Paris*: their social status (whether they were sons of goldsmiths), where they came from (the provinces, Paris or abroad), the exact nature of their apprenticeship (were they simply observers or actual workers?), and more general information on the training (technical, intellectual or artistic) received by the apprentices until they became masters.

Although several pictures of workshops by French engravers survive, notably those of Etienne Delaune of 1576,[1] they do not show clearly the role of the apprentice who is represented either using the *banc à tirer* (a moulding device — a laborious but safe task), or eating an apple whilst watching the other work.

The Statutory Obligations

A few essential points can be drawn from the numerous statutes dealing with apprenticeship:

- only those goldsmiths who owned a shop could take on apprentices and then only one.[2] Although they would generally both lodge and feed their apprentices, and even sometimes provide them with clothing, they would never pay them any wages. The terms of the apprenticeship were fixed in a contract, known as a *brevet*, drawn up by a notary and registered with the guild which would then assign the apprentice to another goldsmith in the event of the death of the goldsmith with whom he had initially been placed.

---

*Translated from French by Isabelle Stone-Cartier.
[1] Bibliothèque Nationale (Bibl. Nat.), Paris: Cabinet des Estampes, Ed 4 a Rés.
[2] The goldsmiths located in the *Grande Galerie du Louvre* were exempted from this restriction (P. Leroy, *Statuts et privilèges du corps des marchands orfèvres-joyailliers de la ville de Paris* (Paris, 1734), p. 47: 'ils peuvent prendre un second aprentis à la sixième année de l'apprentissage du premier.'

- at the beginning of his apprenticeship the boy had to be aged between ten and sixteen years old 'because a child less than ten years old would be incapable of profiting from the instructions given to him, but if over sixteen it was very likely that he would no longer be sufficiently submissive or docile'.[3]
- the apprenticeship lasted for at least eight years, the minimum period required in which to not only train the young man technically, but also to test his *fidelité* et *prudhommie*,[4] that is his faithfulness and his honesty (essential requirements in the precious metals' trade). If the apprentice quit earlier, his parents were obliged to bring him back so that he could continue his work.[5]

These rules however did not apply to the sons of goldsmiths who due to their upbringing were exempt from taking an apprenticeship, as they would have witnessed their fathers at work daily.

From the sixteenth century[6] the recruitment of master goldsmiths in Paris was restricted by the *numerus clausus* — only 300 masters were supposed to work there; if many of them died then access became more open, but if there were too many still practising the guild would give priority to the sons of masters to the detriment of candidates coming from the provinces or from other social or professional backgrounds. This situation existed between 1632 and 1669 when only the sons of Parisian goldsmiths became masters, since the guild then numbered 425 goldsmiths in total.

The practice between 1620 and 1630

It is worthwhile to examine the apprenticeships between 1620 and 1630 since during this period there were many changes and there was much recruitment following the events of October 1621, when a fierce fire broke out on the *Pont au Change* (where most of the Parisian goldsmiths were established) destroying it in only a few hours and killing many:[7] the exact number of goldsmiths who perished in this catastrophe is not known but is estimated at around sixty. Accordingly the number of new masters recruited in the following years increased and this is reflected in the number of apprentices' contracts concluded: around 170 contracts were registered during this short period and most of these diverged greatly from the norms laid down in the statutes.

Who were these apprentices? More than half were Parisian and of these most were the children of the merchant bourgeoisie (candlemakers, tailors, drapers), of trades associated with goldsmiths (burnishers), or neighbours of goldsmiths. Almost a third of them were the sons of goldsmiths who, although exempted from an apprenticeship,

---

[3] 'Car un enfant au-dessous de dix ans ne seroit pas encore en état de profiter des instructions qu'on lui donneroit; et il y auroit à craindre qu'au-dessous de seize, il n'eut plus la soumission et la docilité necessaire.' Leroy, *Statuts et privilèges*.

[4] Lettres patentes 15 October 1597.

[5] Apprentices often and sometimes irremediably quit: in 1625 François Quin reported that his apprentice Jean Garson (aged 17) 'absented himself from the house after living there for four years and was at present in the city of Padua, where his father lives' ('s'est absenté de la maison après y avoir demeuré 4 années...et est à présent en la ville de Padoue où est habitué son père') (Archives nationales (Arch. nat.), Paris, Min centr. CXV, 41).

[6] Edict of Henri II made at Fontainebleau, March 1555.

[7] *Délibérations du Bureau de la Ville de Paris* (ed. H. Surirey de Saint-Rémy), 18 (1953), pp. 123–4.

Fig. 6. Drawing of ornaments in 'cosses de pois' (pea pods) by Gilles Crevon, Paris, 1626. This drawing is a copy of group of ornaments engraved by Isaac Briot after Jacques Caillard, a goldsmith in the Galerie du Louvre.

(Private Collection)

did not overlook training outside their fathers' workshops. However the duration of their training was shorter — from a few months to five or six years depending on the amount of time needed to learn the speciality of their new master.

The other half came either from the countryside around Paris or from provincial towns such as Beauvais, Nantes, Angers, Orléans, Châteaudun, Reims and Péronne, with a third of these again being the children of provincial goldsmiths. In June 1624 Henri Toutin, then aged 12, was placed with the goldsmith Eusèbe Marchant[8] by his father, the engraver and goldsmith Jean Toutin from Châteaudun, and went on to become a master in Paris in 1634. Henri Toutin however is an exception as most of these provincial goldsmiths' sons did not go on to settle in Paris: François Ménard, son of one of the great goldsmiths of Nantes, trained in Paris from 1620 but then returned to Nantes, where he worked until his death in 1654.[9] The fact that the great provincial goldsmiths sent their sons to take their apprenticeships in Paris shows in how much esteem the Parisian goldsmiths were held throughout France.[10]

The practice of sending boys to Paris could have been justified in the learning of techniques that were then being practised only in the capital. For example, at the beginning of the seventeenth century Parisian jewellery was used as a model throughout France, as shown by the engravings of ornaments in *cosses de pois* published by the Parisian editors Moncornet and Le Mercier following the drawn or engraved designs of Parisian goldsmiths (see Fig. 6). As to the working of the metal, the archives record objects described as '*à jour*', that is pierced or perforated, which seems to have been a technique particular to Paris from the sixteenth century onwards; several famous examples survive, such as the cover of a rock-crystal cup belonging to Catherine de Medicis (*c.*1560, Museo degli Argenti, Florence), the censer of the treasure of the Holy Spirit Order (1579–1580, Fig. 7) and the work of François Roberday (Figs. 8 and 9) which show the continued use of this technique . These were the elements that helped to define the 'style of Paris'.

Fig. 7. Censer from the treasure of the Order of the Holy Spirit, Paris, 1579. Silver, pierced and gilded.
(*Musée du Louvre*)

Only a few records survive of foreign apprentices coming to France: these include the son of a merchant from Geneva who spent two years from 1626 with the jeweller

---

[8] Contract of 18 June 1624 (Arch. nat., Min. centr., CXV, 47).
[9] Contract of 4 April 1620 (Arch. nat., Min. centr., CXV, 39). See also, *Les Orfèvres de Nantes, Dictionnaire des Poinçoins de l'orfèvrerie française* (Nantes, 1989), p. 102.
[10] Few sons of Parisian goldsmiths were sent on apprenticeships in provincial towns, athough exceptionally some were as in the case of Jean Simonin who in 1623 was taken on by Pierre Quermezel in Lyons (Arch. nat., Min. centr., CXV, 45).

Fig. 8. Stoup by François Roberday, Paris, 1637. Silver, pierced and chased.
(Private collection.)

Fig. 9. Candlestick by François Roberday, Paris, 1623. Silver, pierced, chased, and cast.
(Musée du Louvre, previously Jourdan-Barry Collection)

Joseph Raillard;[11] two boys from Sedan and Metz,[12] which indicates the artistic vitality of the Duchy of Lorraine during this period; and one Abraham Crasfurd, 'native of Islebourg in Scotland', son of the Scottish goldsmith Daniel Crasfurd, who was placed in 1621 with the goldsmith Marin Collet. In this last example, however, it was almost certainly only to complement his training rather than for a full apprenticeship as he was already aged 21. Further, the contract states that the goldsmith 'promises to make him a better worker than he already is and more likely to earn his living'.[13] Foreigners necessarily hesitated to send young boys, sometimes still children, far away from their countries for such long periods. The largest foreign communities were those of the Flemish, German, Portuguese and Italian journeymen who often settled in France and raised their families there, but rarely placed their sons with Parisian goldsmiths, as these apprenticeships were very expensive. Although never mentioned in the statutes, the fees for an apprenticeship averaged 200 livres but sometimes reached up to 300 livres for an eight-year apprenticeship — equivalent to the annual rent of a shop in Paris. The need for such a considerable financial investment thus inevitably brought about a strong social selection.

[11] Contract of 12 January 1626 (Arch. nat., Min. centr., CXV, 51).
[12] Contract of 20 February 1626 between Jean Brandon, son of the merchant of Torcy near Sedan and the goldsmith Pierre Nolain (Arch. nat., Min. centr., CXV, 51), and contract of 18 January 1650 between Daniel Darragonde, native of Metz and the goldsmith Pierre Baille (Arch. nat., Min. centr., XXI, 157).
[13] 'A le rendre meilleur ouvrier qu'il n'est et plus capable de gaigner sa vye', contract of 23 March 1621 (Arch. nat., Min. centr., CXV, 41).

The amount of the fees, agreed between the boy's parents and the goldsmith, varied on account of the reputation of the goldsmith — all the contracts concluded with the goldsmiths of the *Galerie du Louvre,* who as the royal goldsmiths were highly acclaimed, record high fees. Pierre Delabarre, who was well known for his jewellery designs and his cups which are now in the Prado and the Louvre museums, charged a premium of 300 livres for an apprenticeship,[14] whilst a less renowned goldsmith would have only charged half this sum.

An innovation revealed by the contracts is the division of the apprenticeship into three or even four periods spent with different goldsmiths; this was allowed by the statutes only in the case of the death of the goldsmith, but since it appears so frequently it is likely that this practice was used in other circumstances. This could be explained by the increasing specialisation of goldsmiths divided between those working with either gold or silver and between those making either large or small objects. Thus as each workshop began to specialise in one area it would have seemed logical for an apprentice to train in different workshops so as to learn each of the various specialisations.

The nature of apprenticeships

It is difficult to ascertain the nature of apprenticeships as the statutes deal only with practical aspects and their duration rather than with the precise tasks set for each apprentice. On occasion the archives describe the life of the boy ('le garçon', as he is commonly referred to) but then only indirectly; when there was a dispute between the parents and the goldsmith each party would present their case, as in 1627 when the goldsmith Gabriel Châtelain sacked his apprentice on the basis 'that he did not need an apprentice whose sole task was to open and close his shop'.[15] Reference is occasionally made to the brutality and harshness of the regime imposed by the master, as in 1624 when the apprentice Claude Langlois took refuge with his brother Philippe, a fellow goldsmith, to escape from the 'alleged cruelty' inflicted on him by his master Louis Barre.[16] There are also cases reported of thieving apprentices being dismissed and most contracts reflect the mutual precautions taken by the parents and the goldsmith; for example, it was often stipulated that the boy was only taken on for an initial two-month trial.[17] Some relationships, however, between the goldsmith and his apprentice were excellent, as reported in 1623 when the goldsmith Mathieu Lescot and his wife thanked Jean Marion for looking after their house and for showing such goodwill during an outbreak of plague in Paris.[18]

---

[14] Apprenticeship of Noël Rémy agreed on 20 March 1626 (Arch. nat., Min. centr., CXV, 51); apprenticeship of Charles Féron agreed on 6 July 1643 (Arch. nat., Min. centr., VII, 32).
[15] 'qu'il n'a que faire d'un apprenti qui ne lui peut servir qu'à ouvrir et fermer sa boutique' (Arch. nat., T* 1490[14]; 18 August 1627).
[16] 'prétenduz sévices' (Arch. nat., Min. centr., CXV, 48; 19 November 1624).
[17] This is the case of Georges Pruis, royal goldsmith established in the *Galerie du Louvre,* who took on the son of a goldsmith from Angers for two months, which would only be counted in the period of apprenticeship if he fits the art ('au cas qu'il s'accomode audit art') (Arch. nat., Min. centr., VIII, 625; 27 April 1628).
[18] 'pour le soin qu'il a eu de garder leur maison... et pour la bonne volonté qu'il leur a témoigné en cest accident' (Arch. nat., Min. centr., CXV, 46; 1 August 1623).

The general teaching given by the master on how to work the metal is rarely mentioned, at most it is said that chasing will be taught.[19] Nevertheless, when particular specialities were to be taught they were included in the contract, as in that of 1625 with Nicolas Crochet in which it was specified that the goldsmith would employ his apprentice '*à la seichée et à la dorure*'[20] (burnishing and gilding), both difficult and dangerous tasks which an ordinary apprentice would not normally be expected to perform. The apprentice certainly worked on the metal and participated in making objects as many contracts provided for the reimbursement by the parents of any damages.[21] The unskilful contribution of the apprentice or journeyman can be detected in certain objects now in museums, especially when the work of the master was of excellent quality (for example, the cup of Jean Delahaye, dated 1582–3, now in the Vatican Museum).[22]

The skill of each apprentice can really only be assessed in the making of his masterpiece, which for sons of masters was done at about the age of twenty-one,[23] and for others when around twenty-three.[24] The description of the masterpiece indicates the speciality chosen by the future goldsmith: a goldsmith working with gold might have been asked by the examiners to make a diamond ring,[25] whereas one working with silver might, for example, have had to make a four-pronged silver fork.[26] There exists in the archives a complete file on the masterpiece made by Pierre Baille in 1646 (Fig. 10). It is described as 'a covered cup in the shape of a ciborium'[27] and as the file also contains a sketch drawn in ink, the techniques used can be more easily ascertained: regular hammering, planishing, burnishing, embossing of the cover, and casting of the handles, the finial on the cover and the applied ornaments. This provides a good illustration of the basic techniques used in silversmithing.

Should the apprenticeship be limited to only technical and 'artisanal' training? Obviously not, since draughtsmanship is also an important element in the work of a goldsmith. The apprentice had also to learn to read and write[28] during the early stages

---

[19] 'à cizeller'; extracted from the contracts between Pierre Quermezel and Jean Massé, 28 September 1626 (Arch., nat., Min. centr., CXV, 52).

[20] This apprenticeship was a failure as three years afterwards the goldsmith and the apprentice split, the apprentice having abandoned this speciality ('renoncé à se mesler de l'art de la dorure') (Arch. nat., Min. centr., CXV, 49).

[21] Contract between Pierre Ysambert and the goldsmith Martin Guillot of 28 April 1621 (Arch. nat., Min. centr., CXV, 41).

[22] Vatican Library, Museo Sacro, inv. 1835.

[23] Recall that these became Masters at the end of their theoretical apprenticeship aged between 18 (for those who started aged 10) and 24 (who started aged 16).

[24] After their apprenticeship these had to work in a shop as journeymen for two years before presenting their masterpiece.

[25] Masterpiece of a future goldsmith from Aix-en-Provence in 1657 (Arch. nat., Z^{1b} 157; 17 September 1657).

[26] 'une fourchette d'argent forgée à quatre fourchons'; masterpiece of Adrien Baudeau in June 1675 (Arch. nat., Z^{1b} 652). Another masterpiece in 1677 is described as a silver cup with leaves, foot and handle ('une tasse d'argent à feuilles, pied et anse') (Arch. nat., Z^{1b} 652; 2 June 1677).

[27] 'une couppe couverte en forme de ciboire' (Arch. nat., Z^{1b} 649; file of 17 March 1646). Pierre Baille was a journeyman aged 29.

[28] He must also learn to count, to change money, to evaluate the standard of the metals..., all the skills required generally in business (book-keeping) and in the trade of gold and silver in particular. The theoretical examination to become a master mainly covers these areas.

Fig. 10. Drawing of the model used to make Pierre Baille's masterpiece in Paris in 1646.
(Archives nationales)

of his training: many contracts specify that the master will teach this during the first year of the apprenticeship.[29] The artistic side of the apprenticeship, the draughtsmanship, is at times mentioned: the contract of Antoine Pluyette in 1621 states that his father 'will pay and satisfy the masters who will teach his son portraiture and cast-making',[30] that is to say drawing designs and making plaster moulds and casts. Antoine Pluyette, being the son of a farmer from outside Paris, would never have come into contact before with the artistic movements of his time, in contrast to the sons of masters who had the opportunity, in their family's workshop, to look through printed pattern books and see their fathers' portfolios of drawings. Proof that this training was based on observation and copying can be found in, for example, the ink-drawings made in 1626 by Gilles Crevon during his apprenticeship (see Fig. 6). These were copied from the compilation of engravings by Isaac Briot of the work of the goldsmith Jacques Caillard, which was published in 1629 by Jaspar Isaac.[31] Gilles Crevon, who was to become a master in 1636, was only 17 years old at the time of these drawings but nevertheless shows an excellent mastery of draughtsmanship. Another example, if not of talent then

---

[29] In 1622 the goldsmith Nicolas Mansienne promised to teach reading and writing to his apprentice Pierre Bourbé, son of a stonemason (Arch. nat., Min. centr., CXV, 44; 17 October 1622).

[30] 'Payera et contentera les maîtres qui apprendront à sondit fils à pourtraire et esbaucher' (Arch. nat., Min. centr., CXV, 41; 17 February 1621).

[31] Bibl. nat., Est., Le 40 fol. réserve.

at least of precocious activity, is the engraving in 1646 by the 14 year-old Almot Guyenot, a young apprentice in Dijon and son of a master goldsmith. To practice his skill at engraving he composed a naïve but very detailed view of his father's workshop, in which he included himself.[32] The inspiration of this work was not solely his own but also drawn from patterns for jewellery engraved in 1619 by the goldsmith Jean Toutin.[33] This shows that some apprentices also learnt to engrave.

In conclusion it is the difference in level of training received that should be emphasised; depending on financial or family reasons, it was possible to be taught by the king's own goldsmith or in a little-known workshop. The apprentice could have received a full artistic education or simply learnt to read and write. An example of a high level of training at the beginning of Louis XIV's reign can be found with Pierre de Rosnel, the eldest son of a wealthy Parisian goldsmith. He spent his childhood in his father's workshop but after the latter's death, he was apprenticed by his mother to the goldsmith Antoine Bazille for two years, and then in 1638 with Justin Guyard for six months. During this period his mother made him take drawing lessons from a so-called 'sieur Paul' who taught him portraiture. Afterwards she sent him at her own expense to Rome for a year. After his return, he made his masterpiece and became master in November 1639.[34] The trip to Italy, then more common as part of the training for painters, engravers and sculptors, was however not exceptional in the training of a goldsmith; the Roman archives[35] record forty French goldsmiths as being present in Rome at the end of the sixteenth and beginning of the seventeenth century, and thus show the artistic fervour of the profession.[36]

This evidence of the length of the training, of the technical diversity and of the acquisition of an artistic culture proves (but is it really necessary?) how silver was by no means a minor art during this period. It is only regrettable that the best training was reserved, almost by statute, to the heirs of Parisian dynasties.

---

[32] See H. Schwarz, 'The workshop of a XVII century goldsmith. An unrecorded French print', *Gazette des Beaux-Arts,* 43 (1954), pp. 231–42.
[33] Bibl. nat., Est., Le 52 a Rés, p. 54.
[34] Arch. nat., Min. centr., II, 182: account of the debts owed by Pierre de Rosnel to his mother from his childhood to his wedding, 5 January 1647.
[35] Archivio di Stato di Roma (Archivio notarile).
[36] M. Bimbenet-Privat, 'Les Orfèvres français à Rome, 1500–1650', *Mélanges de l'Ecole française de Rome, Italie et Méditerranée,* 104:2, pp. 455–78.

Training and workshop practice in Zürich in the seventeenth century

HANSPETER LANZ

A drawing by the Zürich painter Conrad Meyer, in the possession of the Goldsmiths' Company in London, shows the interior of a goldsmith's workshop in Zürich in the middle of the seventeenth century (Fig. 11). Besides being an accurate and therefore valuable view of a workshop which shows the work stations, the different operations and the various tools, it also indicates that workshop and shop are combined, and that the three men are quite fashionably dressed. This gives an indication of the social position of a goldsmith in seventeenth-century Zürich, which is confirmed by other

Fig. 11. Drawing of a goldsmith's workshop by Conrad Meyer, *c.*1650. (Diam. 11.9 cm)
(Worshipful Company of Goldsmiths, London)

evidence.[1] Most of the goldsmiths were at some time of their life members of the city council. Some of them held additional official positions which did not allow them to work any more and meant that they had to live as rentiers. The city council was the ruling institution in republican Zürich, and comprised twelve deputies from each of the twelve corporations and eighteen deputies of the Society of the Constaffel. Originally the goldsmiths had to join the noble Society of the Constaffel, but from the late fifteenth century they could belong to any of the corporations according to their family tradition. Families like the Gessner, Heidegger, Holzhalb, Keller, Oeri, and Rahn — from which are descended a number of good goldsmiths of the late sixteenth and seventeenth centuries — were ruling families in Zürich. During the seventeenth century the corporations and the city made it more and more difficult for people from outside to become naturalised, so almost no goldsmith who did not belong to a Zürich family could establish himself. An exception was Hans Heinrich Riva, who was one of the most gifted goldsmiths of the first half of the seventeenth century. He was the man who probably introduced cartilage ornaments and decoration with grotesque masks to Zürich (Fig. 12).

Nevertheless, the local craft was strong enough to develop and to flourish out of its own tradition, to have a dominant position in Zürich and to export throughout Switzerland and even abroad. A few goldsmiths left Zürich and became famous elsewhere: notably Abraham Gessner, who had to leave Zürich because of his commitment to anabaptism; Wolfgang Hauser in London; and Esaias Zurlinden in Nürnberg. From 1600 to 1700 there were about 200 goldsmiths who became masters. At times there were fifty independent goldsmiths' workshops in the city. A goldsmith was allowed to employ one or two apprentices or journeymen at one time in his workshop. If the number of people working or being trained as goldsmiths is compared with the population of

Fig. 12. Nautilus shell cup by Hans Heinrich Riva, 1621. Silver gilt. (Height: 33 cm).
(Schweizerisches Landesmuseum, Zürich)

---

[1] For the following, see Hp. Lanz, J.A. Meier, and M. Senn, *Barocker Luxus. Das Werk des Zürcher Goldschmieds Hanspeter Oeri 1637–1692* (Zürich, 1988), pp. 30–41 and generally E.-M. Lösel, *Zürcher Goldschmiedekunst vom 13. bis zum 19. Jahrhundert* (Zürich, 1983).

Zürich, which between 1600 and 1700 increased from about 8,000 to 12,000, the importance of the craft becomes apparent. It is due, among other reasons, to the economic development of Zürich after the Reformation and to the diligence of the Protestants, who worked hard and invested their earnings rather than spent them.

There was a broad class of well-off craftsmen of all kinds of trades, members of the different corporations who participated in the city government, and some ruling families,

Fig. 13. 'Joseph and his brothers'. Top of a tazza by Hans Rudolf Boller,
c. 1675. Silver gilt.
(Victoria and Albert Museum)

which in the course of the seventeenth century took over the control of government and formed a sort of oligarchy. After 1612, when Zürich re-entered the business of the supply of mercenaries, which had been forbidden by Zwingli, members of the major families became officers in foreign services. Some of them accumulated large fortunes since advantages in trade and business were linked to the procuration of Swiss soldiers, which they had to organise. There was an increasing desire for conspicuous display which was restrained by prescriptions concerning clothing and luxury. It could be said there was a sort of 'hidden' display within the houses and an outburst during the bathing season in nearby Baden where these sumptuary prescriptions were not vigorously enforced. The Victoria and Albert Museum has a Zürich tazza of about 1675 which was offered by the citizens of Zürich to a high-ranking member of the government (Fig. 13). The custom of the quite valuable 'bath-gifts', which could include a piece of silver, is also a sign of wealth and status. Silver in fact was appropriate for a society which was not allowed to flaunt its wealth, and where spending was considered somewhat sinful. It could be used in the private sphere and was at the same time a good investment, at least up to the end of the seventeenth century. From the evidence of inventories, silver vessels are found in ordinary citizens' households and, abundantly, in the household of important men such as Salomon Hirzel, mayor of Zürich, who in 1652 left silver vessels with a total weight of 55 kilograms. His private holdings corresponded approximately to the amount of silver found in the inventories of Zürich corporations and societies. Most of the Zürich goldsmith production was for private or public demand in Zürich and its surroundings. Up to the end of the seventeenth century there was almost no importation of goldsmiths' work. On the other hand, Zürich pieces were commissioned from outside: two of the major pieces of seventeenth-century Zürich silver — a tankard with 'verre eglomisé' panels by Riva and a huge nef by Deucher — were made for dignitaries of Catholic Lucerne, which had quite good goldsmiths at this time. Zürich pieces are found in the Grisons, in central Switzerland, in the Eastern part, in Solothurn and in Bern. Subsequently, Oeri and Werder, both goldsmiths working unusually also with brass and copper, produced work for export, not only throughout Switzerland but also abroad. [2]

How was the craft organised? [3] Besides membership of one of the corporations or of the society of Constaffel, which as already mentioned could vary according to family tradition, the goldsmiths from the middle of the sixteenth century belonged to a guild of their own. This institution had become necessary owing to a sudden increase in the number of goldsmiths in Zürich at the time. In 1562 the first guild book containing the list of the masters from 1525 and of the apprentices from 1560 was started. The task of the goldsmiths' guild was the internal organisation of the craft, the supervision of the training of the new generation, and the enforcement of the various ordinances. These statutes of the goldsmiths and the legislation concerning them, were issued by the government, although after 1562 at the behest of the goldsmiths' guild. After 1621 the guild took over the responsibility for the assay from the city treasurer, with control exercised by four masters. The control was done on the spot using the touchstone method. The cuppellation method was obviously used when there were doubts and subsequently the piece had to be destroyed if it was substandard. Almost no pieces of Zürich goldsmith work with a scraper's mark are known. Every master goldsmith had his own townmark beside his mastermark. An additional warden's mark was struck only towards the end of the eighteenth century.

The required qualification for becoming a master goldsmith was as follows. A young man (no women goldsmiths are known) or rather boy, who was on average 13 to 15 years old, had to be an apprentice for four years. This time could, occasionally, be prolonged up to six years. There were no prescriptions about the way of training, only a general article that the master had to train the apprentice in all required techniques and was not

---

[2] It is not known how these pieces were distributed. In the case of Oeri, it was probably through the textile trade, firstly because of the close link of Oeri with the textile tradesman Andreas Meyer, secondly because of the fact that hilts and belt buckles are types of textile accessories.
[3] See E.-M. Lösel, *Das Zürcher Goldschmiedehandwerk im 16. und 17. Jahrhundert* (Zürich, 1975).

allowed to hide anything. After four years the apprentice was set free and had to travel as a journeyman for another three years. Seven years of training in all was the condition for becoming a master. No masterpiece had to be shown. The young master had to pay a certain amount and had to take the oath.

Although the date, place and duration of apprenticeship of every apprentice in Zürich are known, the towns where they worked as journeyman are generally unknown. Neither for Zürich nor for other European cities do lists exist of foreign journeymen. Only occasionally, or if he got into trouble, was a journeyman registered. So the discussion about further training and transfer of skill has to be held on the basis of little tangible information.

Links with Nürnberg can be supposed in the time of Jost Amman, the famous engraver who was born in Zürich and remained a citizen of Zürich until 1577, although he lived and worked in Nürnberg from 1561 onwards. He was a brother-in-law of the famous goldsmith Abraham Gessner, who worked between 1571 and 1613. The art of engraving and chasing exemplified in the work of Gessner (Fig. 14) and of Hans Peter Rahn, another brother-in-law of Gessner, can be related to a centre like Nürnberg. According to the guild book, Esaias Zurlinden, who later became famous in Nürnberg for his nefs, was an apprentice in the workshop of Hans Peter Rahn in 1593. Related to the connection between Jost Amman and Abraham Gessner is the question of engravings as means of transmission of style or form, or more generally the question of the patterns — in the form of engravings, sketches, or casts — which could be obtained from others and did not always have to be made by the goldsmith himself. These patterns could also be provided by the journeyman and could reflect the stages of his travels during his *Wanderjahre*.

Fig. 14. Cup in the shape of a globe by Abraham Gessner, *c.* 1600. Silver gilt. (Height: 63.5 cm)
(Schweizerisches Landesmuseum, Zürich)

Johann Caspar Füssli in 1769 mentions in his biography of the best artists of Switzerland that the Zürich goldsmith Hans Peter Oeri travelled between 1657 and 1663 as a journeyman, particularly in Germany and Italy, and that he came home charged with art treasures. Probably some of these treasures were patterns. By chance some of the original copper models made and used by Oeri have survived. Belonging to the collection of the Schweizerisches Landesmuseum, they made it possible some years ago to retrace a considerable number of works

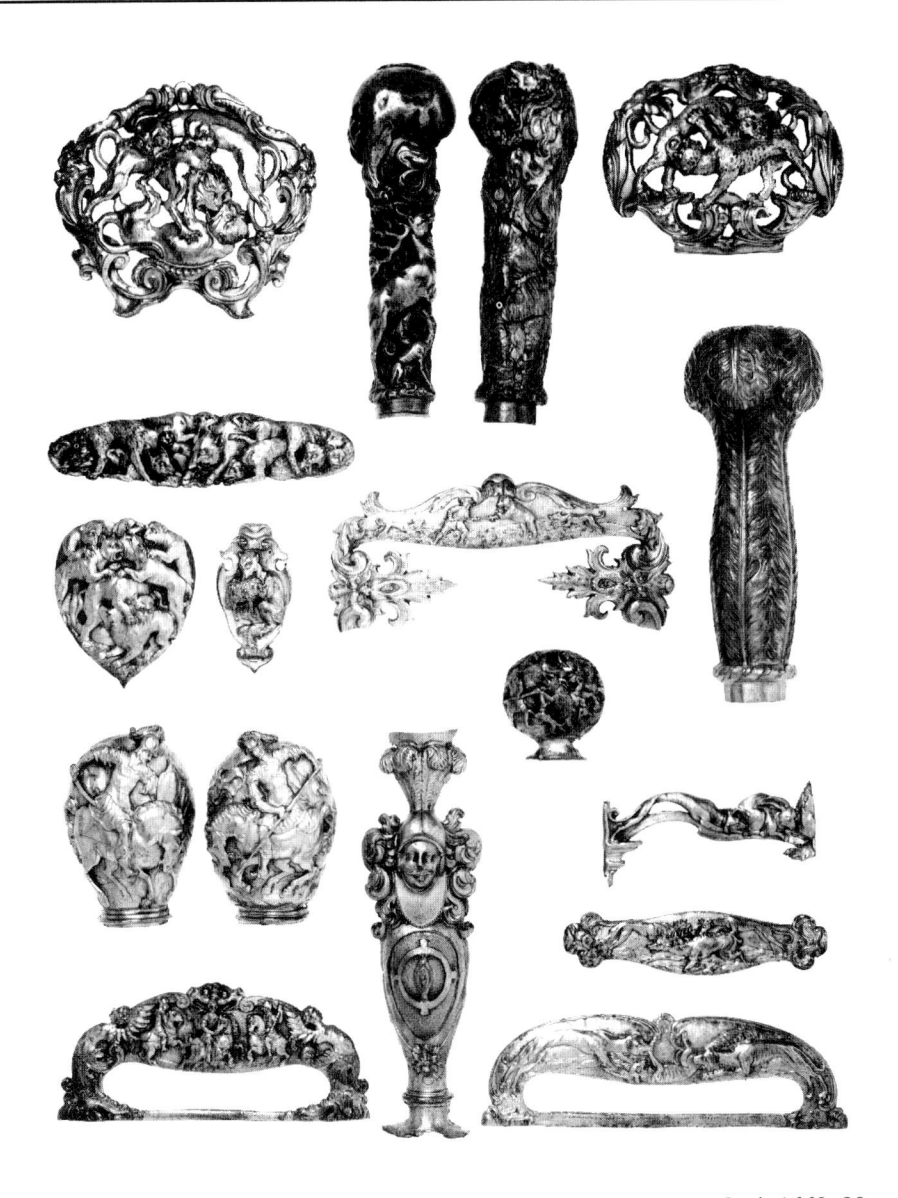

Fig. 15. Seventeen out of thirty-one copper models by Hans Peter Oeri, 1660–80.
(Schweizerisches Landesmuseum, Zürich)

originally made in the Oeri workshop between 1663 and 1691.[4] Twenty-nine of the thirty-one pieces were used for different parts of hilts of swords and for buckles of sword-belts (Fig. 15). The surviving hilts and buckles made after these models are all in bronze which was heavily gilded (Fig. 16). Hans Peter Oeri was probably the most important goldsmith in Zürich of the second half of the seventeenth century. That he was highly regarded during his lifetime can be deduced from the fact that he was allowed to work at the same time in precious and non-precious metal. However, it is

---

[4] Cf. Lanz, Meier, and Senn, *Barocker Luxus*.

Above:
Fig. 16. Clasp by Hans Peter Oeri, 1660/70. Bronze gilt.
(Swiss Private Collection)

Right:
Fig. 17. Tazza by Hans Peter Oeri, 1678. Silver gilt. (Height: 31 cm).
(Schweizerisches Landesmuseum, Zürich)

Fig. 18 Guard of a hilt, c. 1660. Steel.
(Victoria and Albert Museum)

difficult to identify the contemporary influences on the *oeuvre* of Hans Peter Oeri. The report of Füssli does not help as his sources are unknown. The hilts and buckles were generally labelled as 'south German' before their identification. Up to now no specific sketches, engravings or models have been found which could have been used by Oeri. The theme of hunting scenes with different animals is quite common in the European art of the seventeenth century. In his silver pieces Oeri used the cartilage ornaments and grotesque masks then still fashionable in Zürich (Fig. 17) and did not seem to be highly imaginative. One of the buckle models (Fig. 15 bottom left) is somewhat related to a group of sword-hilts generally thought to be French. One of these hilts is in the Victoria and Albert Museum (Fig. 18). The dating of 'around 1660' is confirmed by a painting by Jan de Herdt, in the Kunsthalle Karlsruhe, entitled 'The antique dealer' and dated 1663, which shows a sword with an identical hilt.[5] A hilt on a sketch by Conrad Meyer, which together with other sketches can clearly be related to works of Oeri, again shows a pommel like the one of the V & A hilt. Under these circumstances it may be asked whether Oeri had contacts with France and if therefore Füssli's remarks about Le Brun asking the Keller brothers about Oeri and a possible engagement of his at the court of Louis XIV could have been based on fact. Anyway, through the Keller brothers of Zürich, who held an important position in Paris as cannon founders, and Johann Balthasar who cast the famous equestrian monument of Louis XIV, there were certainly some contacts with France.

As already shown, some of the Oeri works can be related to the sketches by Conrad Meyer and his son Dietrich. The Meyer dynasty of painters, engravers and goldsmiths, going back to Conrad Meyer's father Dietrich Meyer the Elder, painter and engraver, and the tutor of Matthäus Merian the Elder, played an important role in seventeenth-century Zürich. The sketches and engravings over three generations were kept together in the workshop and were used by several family members: besides Conrad and Dietrich the Younger, Johannes, Johannes the Younger, Rudolf, and Hans Jakob, who was a goldsmith like Dietrich the Younger. Further the estate also included sketches and engravings of other artists. It is known, for example, that Merian sent his illustrations and engravings to Dietrich Meyer the Elder as a sign of gratitude because he had learnt a special etching technique from Dietrich. A good part of the sketches and engravings of the Meyer workshop has survived and is kept in the Graphische Sammlung of the Kunsthaus, Zürich. This includes the preparatory sketches for some surviving pieces of various Zürich goldsmiths from the second half of the seventeenth century: Breitinger, Schwyzer and Oeri. The roundel by Conrad Meyer depicting a goldsmith's workshop (Fig. 11) was the source for the extant centre of a lost Zürich tazza whose creator cannot be identified. Many of the scenes engraved or embossed on Zürich pieces of the second half of the seventeenth century go back to Merian (Fig. 13), and some to the battle scenes of Callot. This observation is confirmed by the preparatory sketches for goldsmiths' works in the Meyer estate.

It seems that the Zürich goldsmiths during the seventeenth century became somewhat conservative. Zürich pieces from 1620 to 1680 can be easily identified by a sort of common style based, as far as the ornaments are concerned, on cartilage and grotesque motifs. As there was a common framework to which the contemporaneous stylistic tendencies were adapted, it is difficult to localise the impulse for innovation. Even a personality like Oeri adapted his plate to the main stream. Nevertheless, it can be supposed that a Zürich goldsmith of the seventeenth century had travelled as a journeyman either in Southern Germany, most likely in Augsburg, and/or in places on the Rhine downstream from Basel, even as far as the Netherlands. Except for Dietrich Meyer the Younger, mentioned above, whose travels as a journeyman have recently been reconstructed, the working destinations are not known for any other Zürich goldsmith of the seventeenth century. A sketchbook of Dietrich Meyer covering his time as a journeyman gives not only the stops on his travels but indicates the influences

---

[5] J. Lauts, *Staatliche Kunsthalle Karlsruhe, Katalog alte Meister*, vol. 2 (Karlsruhe, 1966), No. 189. I am indebted to A.V.B. Norman of London for his kind advice.

Fig. 19. Page 4 from the sketchbook of Dietrich Meyer, 1669. Pen and ink wash.
(Zürich Kunsthaus)

Fig. 20. Number 2 from a series of six etchings 'chasses et feuillages...' by
Jean Le Pautre, 1663.
(Zürich Kunsthaus)

to which he was exposed.[6] The sketchbook was started in Zürich in 1669, immediately before his departure. He starts with copying etchings by Jean Le Pautre showing the type of floral scrollwork, which from the 1650s began to circulate from Paris all over Europe (Fig. 19–20). So far it was not put into practice in Zürich which remained in the grip of the old-fashioned cartilage style. Obviously the etchings were around, quite likely in the Meyer workshop. In contrast to Zürich the goldsmiths of Basel from the

[6] Hp. Lanz, 'Das Skizzenbuch II von Dietrich Meyer d.J. (1651–1733) — ein Dokument für den Stilwandel in der Zürcher Goldschmiedekunst um 1675', *Zeitschrift für Schweizerische Archäologie und Kunstgeschichte,* 50 (1993), pp. 263-286.

Fig. 21. Engraving by Dietrich Meyer, 1675–80.
(Zürich Kunsthaus)

Fig. 22. Engraving by Dietrich Meyer, 1675–80.
(Zürich Kunsthaus)

early 1660s switched to the floral style and it was from here that it spread throughout Switzerland. So it is no surprise that Meyer chose Basel as the first stop on his travels in 1670–1. He copied into the sketchbook floral motifs which as patterns for goldsmith pieces were new for him. In 1671–2 he was in Augsburg, then probably in Amsterdam and in 1673–4 back in Basel. During the time of his travels, on the evidence of the sketchbook, he adopted the new development in ornamentation which tended to flatten the floral scrollwork. As a consequence there is a growing emphasis on engraving scrollwork on a plain surface, a tendency which can be seen on Augsburg pieces of the 1670s onwards, but also on Basel pieces.

It seems that Meyer, back in Zürich in 1674, wanted to put into practice the experience of his travels. In the same year he published an engraving with flowers and soon after a suite of engravings with scrollwork, containing flowers (Fig. 21), animals (Fig. 22) and birds respectively. The latter can be related to the suites of Le Pautre and his copyists

Fig. 23. Cup by Hans Conrad Deucher, 1678. Silver gilt. (Height: 46.8 cm)
(Schweizerisches Landesmuseum, Zürich)

Fig. 24. Detail of the foot of cup in Fig. 23.

in Augsburg, Stapf and Reuttimann. From the mid 1670s onwards the first pieces are found in Zürich with high baroque floral scrolls (Figs. 23–24). It seems that Meyer played an important role in this transition from the cartilage style to the floral style. This transition owing to the influence of Meyer could also be an explanation for the divide noticed in Oeri's oeuvre between pieces made from 1665 to about 1680 and those from 1680 to 1691. It is interesting to see that he remodelled some of his most successful hilts such as the deerhunt hilt and the lionshead hilt in the late 1670s. The change is also very evident when the base of the horse by Oeri from the 1660s is compared with that of his horse from the 1680s. Thus, towards the end of the seventeenth century the change in style in the goldsmith production of Zürich can be localised. It seems that Dietrich Meyer and, to as yet an undetermined extent, the atelier Meyer including his father Conrad and his brother Johannes, played a significant role in this development. At much the same time Huguenot goldsmiths who had to leave France in 1685 spread out across Europe and became very influential. Not so in Zürich. Although many Huguenot refugees are known all over Switzerland and among them many goldsmiths, none was accepted as a master in Zürich. Towards the end of the seventeenth century there was a decline in production and consequently also in the number of goldsmiths in Zürich. This crisis was decisive and led to Zürich falling behind other centres like Basel, and those in the French-speaking part of Switzerland like Geneva and Lausanne. The latter saw a tremendous development owing also to the arrival of the Huguenot goldsmiths from France.

Aliens and their impact on the goldsmiths' craft in London in the sixteenth century[1]

Lien Bich Luu

The lavish spending by the church, court, princes, and noblemen led to an enormous demand for goldsmiths' works in early modern European societies. It is little wonder that goldsmithing centres such as Florence, Nürnberg, Augsburg, Utrecht, Milan, Antwerp and Paris emerged where these elite groups clustered. In Paris, with a population of approximately 220,000 in 1600,[2] there were at least 400 master goldsmiths and 500 journeymen and apprentices in 1578.[3] In Antwerp, a city with an approximate population of over 90,000 people in 1566, Ludovico Guicciardini counted at least 124 goldsmiths in 1566.[4] In London, with over 115,000 inhabitants in 1580,[5] there were sixty-eight goldsmiths living in Cheap Ward, and a further twenty in Lombard Street in 1579.[6]

The total number of goldsmiths in London, although likely to have been much greater than eighty-eight, does not seem to have kept pace with the growing demand in the capital, fuelled by its enormous demographic expansion and emergence as a centre of conspicuous consumption where 'men expended the revenues which they had acquired elsewhere.'[7] To tap this rapidly expanding and lucrative market alien goldsmiths from the Continent had streamed to London since the Middle Ages. Their presence was important as 'alien goldsmiths were often the conduit through which awareness of new waves of ornament flowed across the Channel.'[8] In addition, their high level of

---

[1] I should like to thank my supervisor Dr D. Keene, Dr A.C. Duke and D.M. Mitchell for their helpful comments. I plan to discuss many of the issues below more fully in my forthcoming thesis, 'Skills and Innovations: a study of the role of the stranger working community in London c.1550–1600'.

[2] J. De Vries, *European Urbanization 1500–1800* (London, 1984), p. 275.

[3] M. Bimbenet-Privat, *Les Orfèvres Parisiens de la Renaissance 1506–1620* (Paris, 1992), p. 58.

[4] See M. van Gelderen, *The Political Thought of the Dutch Revolt* (Cambridge, 1992), p. 14; G. Marnef, 'Antwerpen in Reformatietijd: Ondergronds Protestantisme in een internationale handelsmetropool, 1550–1577' (unpublished Ph.D. thesis, Leuven University, 1991), Vol. 1, p. 34.

[5] V. Harding, 'The Population of London 1550–1700: a review of the published evidence', *London Journal*, 15 (1990), p. 112.

[6] Goldsmiths' Company, Court Minutes Book (hereafter Court Book) L, Part 2, f. 469. It is difficult to establish the size of the native goldsmithing community in London. In 1509 it has been estimated that there were 89 goldsmiths: 68 in Cheapside and 21 in Lombard Street; and in 1566 there were 108 goldsmiths, 77 of whom had shops in Cheapside, and 31 in Lombard Street. However, the number in Goldsmiths' Row (Cheapside) probably represents a small proportion of the total number of goldsmiths, the majority of whom probably lived outside this area. See J. Evans, *Huguenot Goldsmiths in England and Ireland* (London, 1933), p. 6.

[7] F.J. Fisher, 'The development of London as a centre of conspicious consumption in the sixteenth and seventeenth centuries', in P.J. Corfield and N.B. Harte (eds), *London and the English Economy 1500–1700* (London, 1990), p. 106.

[8] P. Glanville, *Silver in Tudor and Early Stuart England: A Social History and Catalogue of the National Collection 1480–1660* (London, 1990), p. 86.

skill and expertise in particular areas of goldsmiths' work have long been accepted and praised by historians. Ellenor M. Alcorn in her recent article has reiterated a long-held view that:

> although London had a large and prolific goldsmiths' trade, some of the most skilled and innovative craftsmen working for the court in the mid-sixteenth century were aliens. Often at odds with the Worshipful Company of Goldsmiths, which sought to protect its members' interests, the aliens offered specialised skills such as engraving or casting that were in high demand by the most fashionable clientele.[9]

Philippa Glanville has suggested that the nature of craft training and the custom of acquiring experience through the *Wanderjahre* may explain why alien goldsmiths were more skilled than their English counterparts. However, the differentiation of skill among alien craftsmen was probably as large as that between alien and English goldsmiths.

This paper argues, with reference to a group of goldsmiths from Antwerp, that alien goldsmiths cannot be treated as a monolithic group, and that their contribution to the craft in London was determined by where they came from, by the nature of their skills and experience before they arrived, by their motives for coming to London, and by the length of their stay in the City. Some came to seek work and experience, others refuge from persecution. In their own countries it is possible that some alien goldsmiths may not have been regarded as particularly 'skilled'. Therefore, some chose to make London their home where their skills would be valued.

How many alien goldsmiths were working in Elizabethan London; where they came from; how skilled were they; and was there any transmission of skills from alien to English goldsmiths are the central issues which this paper seeks to explore.

Alien goldsmiths in sixteenth-century London

The goldsmiths' craft in London was characterised by two features: the long-standing presence and large number of aliens in the trade. Alien goldsmiths had been active in London in large numbers since the fourteenth century. Reddaway claimed that:

> refugees from the religious persecutions of the second half of the sixteenth century, Flemings and Huguenots, are assumed to be the first great influx of foreign skills into the craft of gold and silver in London. In fact, these men of the previous century must have equalled or surpassed any impact the Huguenots could have made. They may even have provided a proportion of the total goldsmith community greater than that provided by the Huguenots of Elizabeth's reign.[10]

According to a list of 'aliens strangers' dwelling in London, Southwark and Westminster compiled in 1468, there were then 113 alien goldsmiths at work.[11] This figure, however, should be taken as a minimum given the difficulties involved in taking such a survey, and the uncertainty of how the term 'aliens strangers' was defined. It is

---

[9] E.M. Alcorn, ' "Some of the Kings of England Curiously Engraven": an Elizabethan ewer and basin in the Museum of Fine Arts, Boston', *Journal of the Museum of Fine Arts, Boston*, 5 (1993), p. 74.
[10] T.F. Reddaway and L.E.M. Walker, *The Early History of the Goldsmiths' Company 1327–1509* (London, 1975), p. 120.
[11] See Goldsmiths' Company, Court Book A, 1468, ff. 120–21; see also Reddaway and Walker, *Early History of the Goldsmiths' Company*, p. 120.

estimated that in the thirty-five years between 1479 and 1514, 417 strangers swore to observe the Goldsmiths' Company's rules and to obey its jurisdiction: equivalent to an average of twelve aliens being admitted annually.[12] The true figure is likely to have been higher as some strangers did not come to the Company's Hall to obtain a licence to work. Between 1535 and 1562 it is estimated that 232 aliens were licensed to work,[13] that is, on average eight alien goldsmiths were admitted each year. Thus, the total number of aliens working in London was lower between 1535 and 1562 than during the period 1479–1514. The hostility towards aliens, the ban on new immigration, and the expulsion of non-denizen aliens from the capital in 1554 by Queen Mary no doubt affected the existing alien population in London and deterred others from coming.[14] Political, economic and social conditions in the country of origin relative to that in England, however, are also important factors in determining the ebb and flow of immigrants. In the first half of the sixteenth century artisans from the Low Countries, especially from Antwerp, had few causes to migrate to London in great numbers as there was relative political stability, full employment, high wages, and prosperity.[15]

During Elizabeth I's reign the number of alien goldsmiths working in the capital increased again. The Court Minutes Books of the Goldsmiths' Company show that between 1558 and 1598 (with 14 years missing 1578–92), approximately 320 strangers (excluding foreigners[16]), were licensed to work; on average twelve were admitted per year. If we assume that this figure was accurate for the years 1578–92, then probably another 168 alien goldsmiths should be added to the total. In any case, this is a low estimate because some alien goldsmiths were working without licence. Of the seventy-six alien goldsmiths found in the Returns of Aliens in London in 1571 and 1593,[17] for example, only twenty-eight could be found in the Goldsmiths' Company's Court Minutes; the other forty-eight were apparently working without licence. The total number of alien goldsmiths active in London between 1558 and 1598 was probably greater than 500. This level was higher than that in the fifteenth century and the first half of the sixteenth century but because of London's enormous population growth the number of alien goldsmiths was proportionally smaller.[18]

To obtain a licence to work in London alien goldsmiths had to present themselves to the Wardens at the Goldsmiths' Hall, take an oath, pay a fee of three shillings, and

---

[12] Reddaway and Walker, *Early History of the Goldsmiths' Company*, p. 171.
[13] Glanville, *Silver In Tudor England*, p. 92.
[14] A. Pettegree, 'The stranger community in Marian London', *Proceedings of the Huguenot Society*, 24 (5) (1987), pp. 390–402.
[15] See H. van der Wee, *The Growth of the Antwerp Market and the European Economy* (2 vols., The Hague, 1963), vol. 2, pp. 191–99.
[16] A distinction between 'forein' and 'stranger' was made by the Clerk of the Goldsmiths' Company. Both foreigners and strangers were non-free craftsmen. However, 'foreigner' refers to someone from other parts of England, whereas a 'stranger' was someone 'born in a strange country, under the obedience of a strange prince or country'. See I. Scouloudi (ed.), *Returns of Strangers in the Metropolis 1593, 1627, 1635, 1639* (Huguenot Society of London 57; London, 1985), pp. 1–16.
[17] R.E.G. Kirk and E.F. Kirk (eds.), *Returns of Aliens dwelling in the City and Suburbs of London* (Huguenot Society 10, nos. 1–4; Aberdeen, 1900-8), no. 2, pp. 1–139; Scouloudi, *Returns of Strangers*, pp.147–221.
[18] At the beginning of the fifteenth century it is estimated that there were 45,000 people in London. By 1548 there were over 75,000 people living in 122 parishes in London, and by 1600 there were over 200,000. See Harding, 'Population of London', p. 112.

produce a testimonial to show their good behaviour. This possibly entailed a letter from their previous master in Europe with whom they had served or worked. It is curious that the Wardens did not require strangers to show proof of their training but a letter certifying good conduct and behaviour. In 1444 English goldsmiths complained of the great increase in the number of alien goldsmiths, who they argued came to the city because they had been exiled and banished from their own countries 'for diverse offences and trespasses done'.[19] The Wardens of the Goldsmiths' Company, therefore, needed evidence that aliens left their homelands for legitimate reasons, and had come to the city to practise their trade and not to seek refuge from justice. A testimonial was a standard requirement for foreigners to work in other cities. In August 1578, the Wardens of the London Goldsmiths' Company agreed to send a testimonial for the honest behaviour of George Cornelyus, goldsmith, to the town of Middleburg where he was then working.[20] In 1566 the Wardens considered the question of whether stranger free-denizens should be compelled to produce a testimonial.[21] It was decided that a letter of 'denizenship' was sufficient.

Without a 'letter testimonial', the Wardens of the Goldsmiths' Company could simply refuse to allow the strangers to take the oath. Alternatively, the Wardens could permit stranger goldsmiths to work upon the promise by their masters that they would procure such a letter within a period of time, or they could license the stranger to work in the city for a fixed period of time, and after that date to leave if he did not produce his letter. The Wardens, however, realised that the policy did not work, and in November 1574 decided that 'no stranger shall be sworn till he have first brought in and showed his letter testimonial to Master Wardens'.[22] Further, the time letters took to arrive in London from the Low Countries was extremely erratic. And after 1568, in view of the disruption caused to communications by the troubles in the Low Countries, the Dutch Church was sometimes forced to waive the requirement that young people should have written permission to marry from their parents when it was proved that a genuine effort to obtain such a permission bore no fruit.[23] The Wardens of the Goldsmiths' Company therefore were content to accept testimonials from masters in London or from stranger churches. In February 1574/5 Antonie Godmere recommended Peter Drouet to the Wardens, confirming that Peter had been his apprentice in Paris, continued to work with him in London and that he was 'an honest, true man and of good behaviour.'[24] Later in the 1590s stranger goldsmiths brought in 'letter testimonials' from stranger churches. On 8 December 1592, the Dutch Church agreed to give Robte Raynes, a stranger, a testimonial so that he could be admitted into the Goldsmiths' Company.[25]

Of over 320 strangers recorded in the Court Minutes Books, only 64 alien goldsmiths succeeded in obtaining a testimonial. Of these, forty-four, or 69 per cent, came from the Netherlands (twenty-five testimonials, or 40 per cent, alone came from Antwerp),

[19] Goldsmiths' Company, Court Book A, Vol. 2, f. 1.
[20] Goldsmiths' Company, Court Book L, Part 2, f. 410.
[21] Goldsmiths' Company, Court Book L, Part 1, f. 337.
[22] Goldsmiths' Company, Court Book L, Part 2, f. 213.
[23] A. Pettegree, *Foreign Protestant Communities in Sixteenth-Century London*, (Oxford, 1986) p. 227. Letters could reach the Dutch church in three days from Antwerp, but might take up to ten weeks.
[24] Goldsmiths' Company, Court Book L, Part 2, f. 223.
[25] Goldsmiths' Company, Court Book N-O, Part 1, f. 10.

16 per cent from France and 14 per cent from Germany/Rhineland. Was London a favoured destination for many aliens from Antwerp? It has been argued that the majority of journeymen from Antwerp travelled to Italy, Paris, Germany and Spain.[26] However, in view of the political and religious disturbances in Catholic lands such as France in the second half of the sixteenth century, London, with relative political stability, may have been a preferred destination. Communication and travelling networks between London and Antwerp were also relatively easy and quick as since the Middle Ages there had been extensive trading links between these cities.

A number of goldsmiths from Antwerp indicated that they came to London to escape political and religious persecution in the Low Countries. Adrian Brickpott, Peter Noblett, Michael Nowin, Hans Verhagen, all goldsmiths from Antwerp, came to London during the 1560s for the 'sake of religion'. Others such as Nicasius de Glasso, Peter van Doncke, Alexander Dormall, Hans Peniable, also from Antwerp, stated that they came to 'practise their science'. There is no evidence to indicate that they had patrons before coming to London. It is probable that they, like Hans Peniable, came to look for work, and stayed if they found it. Hans Peniable, for example, at first pretended to come to London for 'religion'. When interrogated, he stated his intention to remain in London if he could get work, or else leave for France.[27] In February 1571 he appeared before the Bishop of London and indicated that he had found work, intended to stay and to join the Dutch Church. Kinship networks may have helped the newcomer to find work and integrate. Domenico Sella observes that:

> most emigrants certainly found out about a suitable destination through personal contacts and by word of mouth passed along by relatives or friends who had preceded them and were in a position to report that in a given area opportunities did exist for a given type of skill. Merchants must have played an especially useful role in this respect [as they travelled] a great deal....[28]

Many aliens thus started working with those coming from the same town. Alexander Dormall from Antwerp worked with an Antwerp master, Adrian Brickpott, in September 1566; Henrye van Hover also from Antwerp, worked with Brickpott in 1571; Peter Noblett from Antwerp in October 1568 worked with Denys Volckarts, his brother-in-law, who had in 1562 worked as a foreign master in Antwerp; Guillem van Zwaervelt from Antwerp worked with Denys Volckarts in December 1574; and Lieven Gilleboot from Bruges worked with Volckarts in the same year. Gilleboot may have known Volckarts in Bruges where he originally came from before he moved to Antwerp. Another attraction of London was that the guild was less strict. Here master alien goldsmiths, although unable to retail, were licensed to work by the Company and keep a shop. In Paris, only sons of goldsmiths or Parisian craftsmen were admitted and therefore few foreign goldsmiths could acquire master's status.[29]

---

[26] *Zilver uit de Gouden Eeuw van Antwerpen*, (Antwerp, 1988), p. 24.
[27] Kirk and Kirk, *Returns of Aliens*, vol. 2, p. 156.
[28] D. Sella, 'European Industries, 1500–1700', p. 404, in C.M. Cipolla (ed), *The Fontana Economic History of Europe, Vol. 2: The Sixteenth and Seventeenth Centuries* (Brighton, 1977).
[29] M. Bimbenet-Privat, 'Flemish influence on the goldsmiths' trade in sixteenth-century Paris', given at the Skilled Workforce in Paris 1500–1800 Conference, Paris, April 1993, organised by The Achievement Project, Oxford.

Alien goldsmiths came not only for different reasons, but also with different levels of skills. Adrian Brickpott, for example, had been working as a master goldsmith in Antwerp before coming to London. Denys Volckarts, likewise, started working as a foreign master in Antwerp in 1562 before he is first known to be in London in 1567. In Antwerp the majority of apprentices started their four or more years of training at the age of twelve, followed by several years of *Wanderjahre* with one or more masters, and the majority were twenty-five years of age when they had completed their training.[30] This means that both Brickpott and Volckarts must have had at least thirteen years of training, and several years of experience as masters. Those who came as masters thus were likely to have possessed not only higher levels of skills and experience but also some capital. A crude indication of this is that immediately upon arrival in London, they worked independently and employed servants. Between 1566 and 1571 Brickpott employed at least seven servants, and Denys Volckarts eight servants between 1568 and 1574. Taxation records and wills provide some guide to the wealth of aliens in London. Volckarts was assessed at £25 in the lay subsidy return for 1576.[31] However, his will indicates that his total wealth was far greater. In addition to over £500 of debts which Volckarts instructed his executors to pay, he bequeathed a sum of £5 to the poor of the Dutch Church, and 20 shillings each to his maid and nurse.[32] Others like Peter Noblett and Nicasius de Glas came as journeymen, both of whom worked for an English goldsmith, Mr Louison, in the Ward of Farringdon Within in 1571. Thus, it is important to differentiate different types of alien goldsmiths.

Locations of the goldsmith's trade

The goldsmiths' trade was largely, but not exclusively, concentrated in Cheapside and Lombard Street. In 1501, 119 English members of the Company were recorded paying quarterage. Of these, twenty-two lived in Cheapside, fifteen in Lombard Street and its lanes and alleys, ten in St Martin le Grand, nine in Gutter lane, nine in Ludgate in Fleet Street, seven in St Giles parish, Cripplegate, and seven in Foster Lane. Other areas also mentioned were Westminster, Old Exchange, Wood Street, Cornhill, Bush Lane, Thames Street and Baynard Castle.[33] According to a survey by the Goldsmiths' Company in 1579 the majority of shops in Cheapside, St Matthews Alley (off Cheapside) and Lombard Street were owned by English goldsmiths.

How different were the residential patterns for alien goldsmiths? They tended to congregate in the various 'liberties' and precincts, such as Blackfriars, Westminster and St Martin le Grand. Of the alien goldsmiths mentioned in the Return of 1571, 54 per cent lived in the Wards of Aldersgate, Cheap, and Farringdon within; a quarter lived in the eastern side of Cheap, and 20 per cent lived by the riverside wards. However, alien goldsmiths did not spread themselves evenly within the wards, but clustered in certain parishes and areas. Areas with particular concentration of alien goldsmiths in 1571 were Blackfriars, St Fosters in the Ward of Farringdon Within, and St Martin le

---

[30] *Zilver uit de Gouden Eeuw*, pp. 23–4.
[31] Kirk and Kirk, *Returns of Aliens*, vol. 2, p. 198.
[32] Public Record Office (PRO), PCC 1581 36 Darcy.
[33] Goldsmiths' Company, Court Book A, ff. 387–90.

Grand. These areas were popular among non-freemen as they fell outside the jurisdiction of the City and guilds. In 1580, inhabitants in these areas claimed not only freedom from the jurisdiction of the guilds, but also other extensive privileges. The most important was the freedom to practise their trade.[34]

An additional factor why many alien goldsmiths did not locate in the centre of the goldsmiths' trade — Goldsmiths' Row in Cheapside — was that aliens and foreigners were not permitted to keep an open shop in the City of London. In July 1566, the Court of Aldermen ordered that '...all the foreigners and strangers born to shut up their shop windows that they commonly keep open into the streets and lanes of this City having Lattices before the same...'[35] However, Adrian Brickpott, goldsmith, from Antwerp was licensed in May 1571 by the Court of Aldermen to 'open his shops windows and to work therein, so long as he sets a lattice before his shop windows according to the old orders and laws of this City.'[36] The reason for this is that, according to Philippa Glanville, no passer-by might be tempted to go in and place an order.[37] Furthermore, the Company was concerned to prevent aliens from engaging in retail trade, a privilege reserved to freemen. This may have contributed to the residential segregation of alien and English goldsmiths, and may have reduced the levels of interaction between the two communities.

Alien journeymen goldsmiths

The employment of alien journeymen and servants by English goldsmiths, however, may have been the chief medium whereby skills and ideas were transferred. Evidence from the Goldsmiths' Company's Court Minutes Books shows that of the approximate 400 stranger goldsmiths known to have been working in London between 1547 and 1598, 30 per cent took employment with other aliens, 20 per cent with English goldsmiths, 16 per cent of alien goldsmiths worked independently, 1 per cent had worked for both English and alien goldsmiths; 3 per cent started working as servants and later became independent masters, and the remaining 30 per cent are unknown. Thus, over a fifth of alien goldsmiths had some contact with English goldsmiths. The level of contact increased from earlier periods. According to Reddaway, of the 417 strangers licensed by the Goldsmiths' Company between 1479 and 1514, nearly all took service with aliens already established in the London area.[38]

In the second half of the sixteenth century, a total of sixty-five English goldsmiths employed alien servants, but it is uncertain what proportion of English goldsmiths

---

[34] Inhabitants of the precincts of the Black and White Friars in 1580 claimed several privileges:
  i) to be free from all arrests;
  ii) no search to be made;
  iii) all artificers and craftsmen whatsoever (although they be no freemen of the City) lawfully to exercise their trades, misteries and occupations;
  iv) to be free from all forms of taxation;
  v) to be free from all offices, laws, statutes, customes and ordinances of the City.
PRO, SP12/137/74 April 1580.

[35] Corporation of London Records Office (CLRO), Rep 16/f. 80b.

[36] CLRO, Rep 17/f. 150.

[37] Glanville, *Silver in Tudor England*, p. 86.

[38] Reddaway and Walker, *Early History of the Goldsmiths' Company*, p. 171

these formed. However, it is important to note that of these sixty-five English goldsmiths, almost 20 per cent had shops in Goldsmiths' Row. Edward Gylberd, for example, who owned the 'Ship' in Cheapside, employed George and Melchior Pyntter in 1566, John Grillett in 1566–7, and Wolryke Oste in 1571. Richard Hanberrie who owned the 'Maidenhead' in Cheapside, employed John Holteman and Amery Le Boucq in 1567.

Of the forty-two Antwerp goldsmiths, eleven, or over 25 per cent, are known to have worked with English goldsmiths at some point of their stay in London.[39] Was there any transmission of skills or ideas? It has been suggested that alien goldsmiths working with English masters were hired to 'work on their piece', the goods would be submitted for assay by their English employer and would be struck with his mark. In later periods it was a frequent complaint on the part of some London goldsmiths that others would for a fee take a piece made by a foreigner to Goldsmiths' Hall for marking and assaying, and so encouraged foreigners to set up on their own instead of seeking employment under an English master.[40] Working 'on their own piece' suggests that there was little interaction between alien and English goldsmiths in the manufacturing process, whereby ideas and skills may have been exchanged, learned and transmitted, as the goods were made independently by strangers and were merely retailed by English goldsmiths. The Company, however, forbade its members to 'receive any stranger into his house to work upon his own goods',[41] yet there were persistent offenders. The extent of this practice is unknown, and only when the offender was caught did the evidence came to light. On 2 April 1563 Rondell, 'goldsmith and clock maker promised to set strangers... to work with him as *servants* and *not as masters*'.[42] On 12 May 1567 it was reported that Henrie Watson, a foreign goldsmith, had two strangers working with him upon their own piece.[43] John Mathue, an English goldsmith, likewise employed two strangers in his house working upon their own piece in 1574.[44] Punishment for this offence could be severe. On 6 December 1574 Nichas Zeghar, a stranger, was fined £3 for allowing a stranger to work in his house upon his own piece, and having no letter testimonial.[45] In December 1550 Thomas Flynte and Fraunces Vyncent, and the strangers involved, were sent to prison.[46] This was clearly viewed by the Company as a serious offence.

Evidence suggests that stranger goldsmiths were employed also by those who had little skill in the goldsmith trade. In 1567 James Vanderaste from Antwerp was employed

---

[39] James Couman, for example, from Antwerp, worked with Alb. Whitlock in October 1567; Nicasius de Glasso worked with Mr Bushe in 1568, and later in 1571 with Mr Louison; Peter van Doncke also worked with Mr Louison in 1571; Hans Franke with Harry Coldwell in July 1548; Marcus Hay with John Ashemore; Dauid Hellynk with Mr Grene in St John Zacharye parish in 1571; Christopher Hicks with Thomas Pope (in Lombard Street) in March 1566; Joose van Mynden with Henrie Courte in November 1567; James Vanderaste with Thomas Southwarke in September 1567; Josep van Dueren with Thomas Flynte in February 1574; and Hans Verhagen with William Bowyer in September 1567.

[40] J.F. Hayward, *Virtuoso Goldsmiths and the Triumph of Mannerism, 1540–1620* (London, 1976), p. 302.

[41] 1469 Ordinance, Reddaway and Walker, *Early History of the Goldsmiths' Company*, p. 249.

[42] Goldsmiths' Company, Court Book K, Part 1, f. 217.

[43] Goldsmiths' Company, Court Book L, Part 1, f. 353.

[44] Goldsmiths' Company, Court Book L, Part 2, f. 204.

[45] Goldsmiths' Company, Court Book L, Part 2, f. 216.

[46] Goldsmiths' Company, Court Book GHI, f. 120.

by Thomas Southwark in Cornhill, who had 'some skill in the workmanship of goldsmithry, keeps open a goldsmiths shop under the widow his mother, and is not yet free himself, but intends to be made free of the Merchant tailors by his father's companie.'[47] This suggests that those without the necessary skills could provide the capital and employ skilled labour to work in their shop.

In summary, there appears to have been increasing contact between alien journeymen and English goldsmiths in the second half of the sixteenth century. However, it is difficult to establish whether this led to any diffusion of skills or not, as aliens were set to work on their own piece, suggesting that they completed a piece of work independently and may not have involved English goldsmiths in the production.

Diffusion of skills through apprenticeship

The other main channel through which skills could be diffused from aliens to the indigenous population was apprenticeship, and aliens were often under pressure to take English apprentices. As early as 1444 English goldsmiths complained that aliens and freemen aliens in Southwark and Westminster took as their servants 'aliens born and never of English nation' causing unemployment among many native workmen. It was therefore proposed that no alien goldsmith was allowed to take, keep, admit or receive an alien into his service or to be apprentice whilst there were English servants or apprentices available. If aliens did not abide by such rules, they were to be fined 40 shillings and sent to prison.[48] In the second half of the sixteenth century the Goldsmiths' Company Court Minutes Books record only five or so English apprentices bound to alien goldsmiths. This suggests that although aliens were working in large numbers in London, they did not play a crucial role in training the future generation of English goldsmiths — the apprentices.

Firstly, their transitory stay in the capital, no doubt, meant that it was impossible to bind apprentices to them for a fixed term of several years. Some of them, however, were also unqualified to teach others the skills, as many of them were journeymen on their *Wanderjahre* whose purpose here was to accumulate and gain experience from several masters, a career building step, in order to promote their fortunes elsewhere. Of the forty-two goldsmiths from Antwerp, at least seven returned to that city and can be traced in the records there. All of these, except Nicholas Lardenoys, came to London as journeymen as part of their *Wanderjahre* to accumulate experience. These stayed in London between a few months and twelve years. Peter van Doncke stayed in London for only a few months before returning to Antwerp, Cornelius van Leemputte stayed in London for approximately five years before starting work as a master in Antwerp, Peter Noblett seems to have been in London for twelve years before returning to Antwerp in 1580.[49] Others stayed permanently in London. John Bearle in 1593 indicated he had been in the capital for twenty-one years; Nicasius de Glas first known to be in London in 1568, stayed in London for at least thirty-one years.

---

[47] Goldsmiths' Company, Court Book L, Part 1, f. 368.
[48] Goldsmiths' Company, Court Book A, ff. 2–3.
[49] Antwerp Stadsarchief, Goud- en Zilversmeden Ambacht: Accounts Book 1564–92, A4487; miscellaneous documents 1400–1600, A4488.

Secondly, the supply of apprentices was curtailed as the Wardens of the Goldsmiths' Company were concerned that 'when the same apprentices shall come to their freedom, they shall not be able (being so many in number) to live one by another specially the company being already (besides foreigns and strangers) fully replenished with journeymen and young men newly set up.' An order was therefore issued in August 1563, allowing liverymen to keep up to two apprentices at a time, householders one apprentice and those admitted to the Company as brothers for less than three years were prohibited from having apprentices.[50]

Thirdly, it was probably more expensive to bind English apprentices to alien goldsmiths as apprentices had to be bound first to freemen (English) goldsmiths before they could be turned over to strangers. On 8 August 1565 the Company declared that,

> no stranger or foreigner of this occupation shall take any freemens children of London to be their apprentices by the statute of Winchester or otherwise whereby they may by any means be instructed in the art of goldsmithrie. But shall take and teach in the said art only such freemens children as be first apprentices to freemen of this companie after the order of London and to them enrolled.[51]

Between 1590 and 1600, 670 apprentices were enrolled, on average sixty-seven per year.[52] Yet, the Return of Aliens of 1593 shows that of the fifty-two English servants employed by alien goldsmiths only two were apprentices. Institutional barriers combined with the transitory stay of alien goldsmiths meant that they did not play an important role in the training of the future generation of goldsmiths in London.

Conclusions

Alien goldsmiths had been working in London in large numbers since the Middle Ages. Although the number of alien goldsmiths rose during Elizabeth's reign, this increase did not keep pace with London's population growth. There were in fact proportionally more alien goldsmiths in the fifteenth century than in Elizabethan London.

The most skilled and experienced alien goldsmiths were those who came as masters. They worked independently and apparently had little contact with English goldsmiths. It is difficult to establish what impact they had on the craft, but what seems certain is that they did not play an important role in the training of English goldsmith apprentices.

The alien journeymen, on the other hand, had more contact with English goldsmiths. However, these were not necessarily the most skilled and experienced. Some came to accumulate experience, and it was not uncommon for them to work with someone from the same town. A high proportion returned to their homeland and built up their careers there. Furthermore, they were often employed to work on their own pieces, and in the process of making these there may have been little contact with their masters.

---

[50] Goldsmiths' Company, Court Book K Part 1, f. 233. See Challis, n. 52 below. This order did not seem to affect the enrolment of apprentices: 474 apprentices were enrolled between 1560 and 1570; 459 apprentices between 1570 and 1580.
[51] Goldsmiths' Company, Court Book K Part 1, f. 291.
[52] C. Challis, 'Training and workshop practice in England in the seventeenth century', paper delivered at the 'Innovation and Skill in Goldsmiths' Work' Study Day, Victoria and Albert Museum, 24 November 1993.

Balances and goldsmith-bankers: the co-ordination and control of inter-banker debt clearing in seventeenth-century London

STEPHEN QUINN

In the seventeenth century, demandable paper debt acted as a medium of exchange that saved transaction costs relative to moving, protecting and assaying coin or bullion. Early modern Europe used bills of exchange to avoid shipping bullion.[1] The savings in transaction costs by using bills of exchange or other paper debt were increased with the introduction of transferable debt[2] and of institutions to clear off-setting balances. Evolving from the medieval fairs, exchange banks such as Amsterdam's were the premier international credit institutions of the seventeenth century. The Amsterdam Exchange Bank (Wisselbank) established low cost, par clearing of intra-bank debts and played a large role in Holland's commercial success. In the second half of the seventeenth century, goldsmith-bankers introduced systematic debt clearing in London.

The goldsmith-bankers' system of clearing included domestic notes along with bills of exchange. In the seventeenth century, promissory notes (paper promises to pay, bank notes) and drawn orders (cheques) were in common use. Both bank notes and cheques were referred to simply as 'notes'. London's system allowed the public to write cheques or pass bank notes that would be accepted and cleared at par by a network of goldsmith-bankers. The widespread acceptance of demandable debt by bankers increased the value of goldsmith-banker notes and cheques. Increased public valuation occurred for two reasons: mutual banker acceptance expanded the circle of uses to which the medium of exchange could be put; and acceptance at par meant users did not have to stay abreast of the current discounts, so transaction costs were again reduced.

With an acceptance network, goldsmith-banker notes and demand accounts held a higher value and circulated more widely than they otherwise would. With improved acceptance raising the value of demandable debt by the public, each banker could issue more notes. Assuming notes returned to the goldsmith-banker in a random way, the note-issuing banker would enjoy a diminishing variance of repayments relative to debt issued. The chance of either all of his notes or none of his notes appearing for repayment on

---

[1] H. van der Wee, 'Monetary, Credit and Banking Systems', *Cambridge Economic History of Europe, The Economic Organisation of Early Modern Europe* (Cambridge, 1977), vol. 5, pp. 290–393; E. Kerridge, *Trade and Banking in Early Modern England* (Manchester, 1988).

[2] See S. Quinn, 'Banking before the Bank: London's unregulated goldsmith-bankers, 1660–1694' (unpublished Ph.D. Thesis, University of Illinois, 1994), chapter 1.

any one day fell as the goldsmith-banker extended more credit. More stable, predictable balances meant bankers could float still more notes. Likewise, demand deposits with bankers were of more value as the circle of cheque acceptance grew.

Unlike the great exchange banks on the Continent, London's system for clearing notes (bank notes and cheques) was not centralised into one bank or clearing house. London's goldsmith-bankers and merchants knew how exchange banks worked, and many pamphleteers called for the establishment of a government-backed bank.[3] However, England's kings had forced loans and confiscated property during the first half of the seventeenth century.[4] Moreover, Charles II would default (the 'Stop of the Exchequer') on most government debt in 1672. Until the Glorious Revolution and the placing of the king within the Common Law, the Crown could not be trusted to respect property rights.[5] The same threats that prevented a state-chartered public bank endangered any private endeavour. Securing a legal structure of an exchange bank in London would also have inhibited the accumulation of capital, even without fears of confiscation. Firms were limited to ownership by individuals and partnerships. With no limited liability, an extended partnership in which all members had to deposit specie 'up front' would have entailed tremendous risk. To trust any individual with the same money could have been riskier still.

Rather, each goldsmith-banker cleared with each other banker on a direct, individual basis. Moreover, the goldsmith-bankers avoided depositing large sums with each other by routinely creating overdrafts. Rather than demand positive balances as a precondition for note acceptance, London's goldsmith-bankers regularly accepted other bankers' notes without covering deposits being on hand. Acceptance of unbacked demandable debt created deficits. The goldsmith-bankers limited their exposure by restricting overdraft creation to notes presented by third parties. Bankers then managed existing overdrafts by closely monitoring debts and quickly clearing balances.

Goldsmith-bankers had incentives to join the clearing network. Customers might abandon a lone banker. London's merchants sought bankers for convenience and liquidity.[6] A merchant who had to go to another banker on Lombard Street to cash a cheque might just move his whole account there. Also, bankers outside the system missed the expanded note circulation that came with membership. Likewise, an individual banker attempting to introduce fees or interest charges would face potential ostracism from his fellow bankers or loss of customers depending on who the goldsmith-banker tried to charge.

Wanting in and getting into the clearing network, however, were different things. Most new goldsmith-bankers were filtered through the process of apprenticeship to established goldsmith-bankers. Apprenticeship limited access to the ranks of an 'old boy' clique within the Goldsmiths' Company of London. Once a member, most of the

---

[3] M.H. Li, *The Great Recoinage of 1696 to 1699* (London, 1963); K. Horsefield, 'The "Stop of the Exchequer" Revisited', *Economic History Review*, 35 (1982), pp. 511-528.

[4] R. Ashton, *The Crown and the Money Market, 1603–1640* (Oxford, 1960).

[5] D. North and B. Weingast, 'Constitutions and commitment: the evolution of institutions governing public choice in seventeenth-century England', *Journal of Economic History,* 49 (1989), pp. 803–832.

[6] H.G. Roseveare, 'The advancement of the King's credit 1660–1672' (unpublished Ph.D. Thesis, Cambridge University, 1962).

bankers in the clearing system lived within or close to Lombard Street. Over the course of the Restoration era, clearing also developed among the growing network of goldsmith-bankers in the vicinity of Fleet Street and the Strand.[7]

Co-ordination built on apprenticeships coupled with overdraft control through rapid note clearing provided a framework for a system of decentralised inter-banker clearing in seventeenth-century London. The goldsmith-banker system of clearing was a fundamental break from the system of exchange banking well established in the Low Countries, Italy and elsewhere. London's system of debt clearing was not centred in a clearing house or central bank. The goldsmith banker himself was owed for each overdraft until the note was cleared. In contrast, the Amsterdam Wisselbank only accepted a note if the offsetting credit was already on deposit.

This paper examines the demandable debt clearing system of London's goldsmith-bankers in quantitative terms through the accounts of Edward Backwell. Backwell's ledgers run from March 1663 until March 1672 but miss twelve months of records from September through December 1663 and March through December 1665.[8] While one banker's clearing accounts with his fellow bankers cannot portray the entire system, Edward Backwell's accounts do detail his inter-banker balances. Earlier writers have interpreted Backwell's extensive relations with other goldsmith-bankers as evidence that the goldsmith-banker was a 'banker's banker'. R.D. Richards concluded that Edward Backwell, 'was undoubtedly both the central or reserve bank and the clearing house of the post-Restoration period. [Backwell's bank] was the indispensable precursor of the Bank of England, a precursor which was of paramount importance in this outstanding era of English economic expansion.'[9]

Although the network of goldsmith-bankers was an 'indispensable precursor of the Bank of England', Edward Backwell was not a clearing house. At least nineteen goldsmith-bankers held accounts with Backwell over the decade from 1663 to 1672, but they did not clear with each other *through* Backwell.[10] Rather, each banker mostly cleared only his own and Backwell's notes with Backwell.

Occasionally Backwell's clearing accounts would involve a third banker. To argue these infrequent entries constituted a clearing house would suggest that *all* goldsmith-bankers, besides and unlike Backwell, issued very few notes. The author knows of no reason to assume that Backwell was special in regards to note issuance. Moreover, no argument has been presented by earlier writers as to why other bankers would accept Backwell's notes but not those of other prominent bankers. Such a system would constrict

---

[7] D.M. Mitchell, ' "Mr Fowle, Pray Pay the Washwoman": The Trade of a London Goldsmith-banker, 1660–1692', *Business and Economic History*, 23 (1994), pp. 27–38.
[8] Royal Bank of Scotland Archives, London, EB/1-9: Edward Backwell, Ledgers J (March 1663 to March 1663/4), K (March 1664 to September 1664), M (September 1664 to March 1664/5), O (January 1665/6 to December 1666), P (January 1666/7 to March 1667/8), Q (March 1668 to March 1668/9), R (March 1669 to March 1669/70), S (March 1670 to March 1670/1), T (March 1671 to March 1671/2).
[9] R.D. Richards, *The Early History of Banking in England* (London, 1929), p. 30.
[10] Backwell also had regular clearing transactions with the money-scrivener firm of Morris and Clayton. The money-scriveners were substitute financial intermediaries specialising in mortgages and formal deeds; see F. Melton *Sir Robert Clayton and the Origins of English Deposit Banking, 1658–1685* (Cambridge, 1986). Their accounts with Backwell demonstrate that the scriveners and goldsmiths both benefited from participating in a system of mutual debt acceptance.

Fig. 25. Edward Backwell. Anonymous engraving.
(Worshipful Company of Goldsmiths)

the circle of note acceptance to the detriment of everyone except Backwell. Instead, evidence points towards a system of dispersed clearing. For example, Child was a small but growing West End banker rather than the Lombard Street giant that Backwell was, yet the ledgers of Sir Francis Child, like Backwell's, record regular clearing activities with a number of goldsmith-bankers.[11]

This paper puts forward a new interpretation of Edward Backwell as an important member in a web of banker-to-banker clearing arrangements. Each goldsmith-banker had an incentive to join the network in order to satisfy liquidity conscious customers and expand note circulation. Acceptance of notes by overdrafts spared each member establishing covering balances at all the other bankers' shops. The banker carrying the interest-free negative balances was the least cost monitor of overdrafts (since they were in his bank) and had a clear incentive to monitor accounts and clear deficits promptly. On a system-wide level, each banker knew that every other two banker clearing relationship had a similar motivation for expeditious clearing, so the risk of abusive over-issue of notes was contained by the incentive compatible structure of the network.

I Backwell's Inter-Banker Balances

Edward Backwell was an early modern banker of the largest order.[12] Having served as an apprentice to the important Cromwellian goldsmith-banker, Sir Thomas Vyner, Alderman Backwell became a banker to members of the restored royal family, the customs revenue, numerous crown agents including Samuel Pepys, the East India Company and hundreds of merchants, gentry, professionals and others.[13] From his shop, the Unicorn on Lombard Street, Backwell ran a diverse business.

> Interest was paid on deposits; loans were supplied; bills of exchange, tallies and various types of Treasury-Exchequer payment orders were discounted; promissory notes, which circulated freely, were issued; cheques were used; bullion was bought and sold; foreign coins were changed; systematic accounts were kept in special ledgers.[14]

The scope and scale of Backwell's bank make him a central player in the goldsmith-banking system of the 1660s, the first decade with surviving quantitative evidence of inter-banker clearing activity. Backwell's transactions with his fellow goldsmith-bankers must be interpreted from the perspective of Backwell's prominence and breadth of activities.

---

[11] Royal Bank of Scotland Archives, London, CH/194: Sir Francis Child, Customer Ledgers; Mitchell, 'Mr Fowle', p. 28; S. Quinn, 'Tallies or reserves? Sir Francis Child's balance between capital reserves and extending credit to the Crown, 1685–1695', *Business and Economic History,* 23 (1994), pp. 39–51.

[12] F.G. Hilton-Price, 'Some account of the business of Alderman Edward Backwell, goldsmith and banker in the seventeenth century', *Transactions of the London and Middlesex Archaeological Society,* 6 (1890), pp. 191–230; D.K. Clark, 'Edward Backwell as a Royal Agent', *Economic History Review,* 9 (1938–39), pp. 45–55; R.D. Richards, 'The Stop of the Exchequer', *Economic History: Supplement to the Economic Journal,* 2 (1930), pp. 45–62.

[13] Clark, 'Backwell as Royal Agent', pp. 45–55.

[14] R.D. Richards, 'A pre-Bank of England English banker — Edward Backwell', *The Economic Journal* (1928), pp. 335–355.

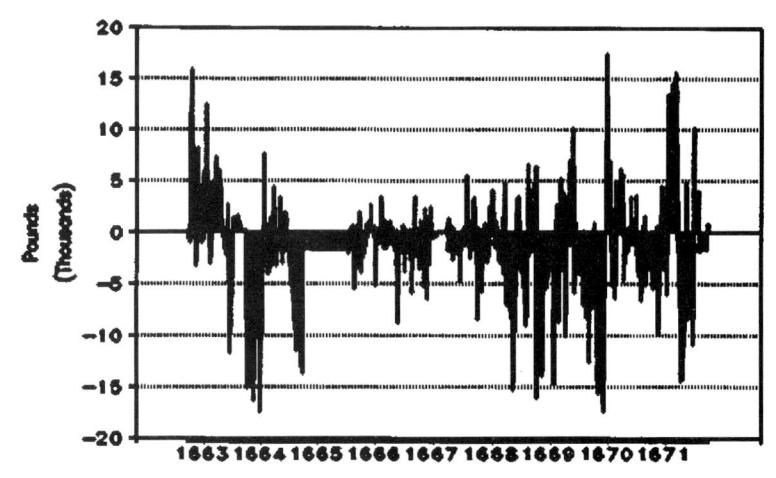

Fig. 26. Balances of all bankers with Backwell except Vyner

TABLE 2
Distribution of daily balances for all bankers on Edward Backwell, January 1663 to March 1672[1]

	By number of observations	By Standard Normal Distribution
Minimum = –£17,487		
10%	–£7,731	–£12,349
33%	–£2,038	–£3,340
50%	Median = –£813	Mean = –£1,445
66%	–£16	£449
90%	£3,450	£9,459
Maximum = £17,476		

[1] Distribution excludes missing observations for January–March 1663/4 and March–December 1665.

Fig. 26 presents the aggregate daily balance of nineteen goldsmith-bankers with Edward Backwell.[15] Each goldsmith-banker's account with Backwell was encoded and calculated separately and then summed. At various times Backwell held both positive and negative balances relative to his fellow goldsmith-bankers with a daily

---

[15] Sundays have been excluded from Fig. 26 and the rare Sunday transaction has been moved to the prior Saturday. The sample includes the earliest generations of goldsmith-bankers: John Colvill, John Lindsay, John Mawson, Francis Meynell, John Portman, Jeremiah Snow, George Snell, Thomas Vyner (Fig. 27), and Robert Welstead. Thomas Cook, John Hinde, Benjamin and Edmund Hinton, Joseph Horneby, Thomas Kirwood, Thomas Pardo, Thomas Row, Bernard Turner and Thomas Williams all began accounts with Backwell after March 1663. Over the run of Backwell's ledgers, Vyner, Colvill and Meynell died. As noted above, Thomas Vyner's shop was passed into the hands of his nephew Robert. Francis Meynell's business was carried on by his brother Isaac. Both transfers provided a continuation of inter-banker clearing. John Colvill was survived by his widow Dorothea Colvill who settled many affairs in her account with Backwell. Finally, only those that have been identified by other sources (see A. Heal, *London Goldsmiths* (London, 1935); F.G. Hilton-Price, *A Handbook of London Bankers* (London, 1890); and F.G. Hilton-Price, 'Some notes on the early goldsmiths and bankers', *Transactions of the London and Middlesex Archaeological Society*, 5, (1881), pp. 255–281) as goldsmith-bankers have been listed. As yet unknown bankers are not included, so the sample is biased towards exclusion.

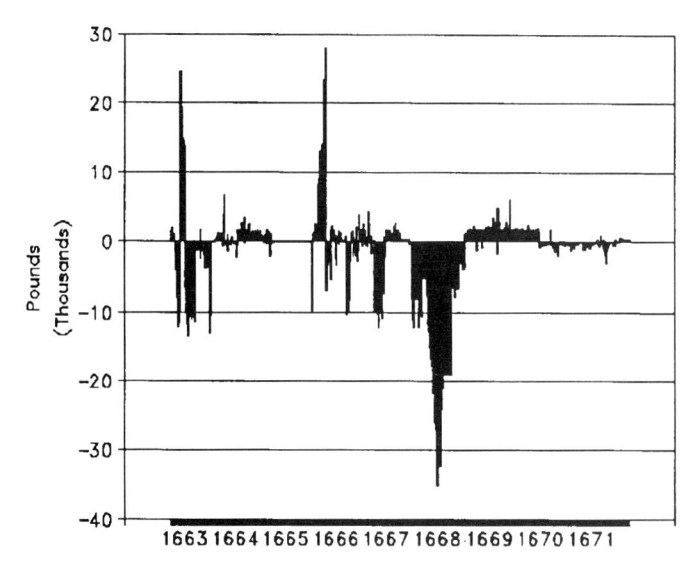

Fig. 27. Balances of Thomas and Robert Vyner with Backwell

mean of −£1,445 over the 2,511 day sample.[16] The series had a standard deviation of £4,700. As Table 2 shows, the median total banker balances held by Edward Backwell was −£813 and considerably higher than the mean.

Backwell's accounts with his fellow goldsmith-bankers mingled clearing with other types of transactions. The accounts include loans and bullion sales between Backwell and his colleagues. These effects are separated out for a sample of three bankers in Section III (below), but the values in Fig. 26 remain largely a mixture of direct loans and clearing overdrafts. However, a few extreme inter-banker relationships have been removed from Fig. 26.[17]

Because of their special relationship, Fig. 26 excludes the account of Sir Thomas and Sir Robert Vyner from Backwell's total balances with all bankers. Most of Backwell's very largest daily balances were a result of his special relationship with the shop of his former master Sir Thomas Vyner and Sir Thomas' nephew, Sir Robert Vyner. Sir Robert Vyner assumed full proprietorship of the Vine after 1665. Both Vyners were men of great importance — Sir Thomas received Oliver Cromwell's first grant of knighthood and Sir Robert was a personal friend and financier to Charles II.[18] Fig. 27

---

[16] Although graphed, balances from 1 January 1663/4 to 24 March 1664 and from 25 March 1665 to 31 December 1665 are not included in the summary statistics.

[17] Adjusting Fig. 26 (as described below) lowered the daily mean from an unadjusted −£1,337 to −£1,445. The variance of balances, however, fell substantially from Backwell's unadjusted position of £11,008 to £4,700. Besides Vyner, Fig. 26 also excludes extraordinary spikes in the balances of Sir Francis Meynell and Thomas Row. On 18 April 1663, Meynell was credited by Backwell for £34,666.13s.4d on behalf of money received by the sale of Dunkirk. In August 1670, Row deposited over £30,000 in foreign coin with Backwell. In January and February 1671, Row was repaid by the East India Company for whom Backwell was their banker. Both outliers have been removed from Fig. 26 to highlight the remaining transactions.

[18] D.K. Clark, 'A Restoration goldsmith-banking house: The Vine on Lombard Street', *Essays in Modern English History* (Cambridge, Mass., 1941), pp. 3–47.

plots the daily balances of the Vyners with Backwell and reveals that the Vyners occasionally ran balances of over twenty and even thirty thousand pounds.

In the extreme, the summer of 1668 saw Vyner's debt reaching £35,000 by late June. In 1667, after the disastrous Second Dutch War, depositors ran on Vyner who was owed at least £1,500,000 by the Crown.[19] In 1668, depositors remained uneasy and the Crown pressed for more funds with threats of withholding interest payments.[20] During that difficult summer, Backwell appeared to have provided Vyner with substantial credit.[21]

After excluding Backwell's unique relationship with the Vyners, Backwell's daily inter-banker clearing of short run debt can be viewed as a process of inventory control. In contrast to stories that involve one firm's positive balances,[22] the reciprocative acceptance of debt between goldsmith-bankers involved overdrafts and two optimising parties. Bankers holding accounts with Backwell sought to minimise non-interest bearing credits but had no personal compulsion to pay off free overdrafts. Backwell, in contrast, desired to lessen debits (interest free loans) but not credits.

Together, the bankers created an incentive compatible arrangement to control balances while maintaining the benefits of clearing. In the Miller-Orr model of cash management, a firm holding a demand account weighed the cost of moving funds out of the account against the opportunity cost of leaving the funds on deposit without accruing interest. The banker holding accounts with Backwell had the same incentive to minimise positive balances with Backwell. Backwell's colleagues, however, had no inclination to clear interest-free overdrafts.

Unlike his account holders, Backwell did have an incentive to minimise the cost of holding negative balances. It seems that Backwell accepted overdrafts because his compatriots tolerated negative balances in Backwell's accounts with them. Backwell was constrained in limiting negative balances because his fellow bankers would in turn limit his overdrafts with them. The mutual elimination of overdrafts between the bankers would destroy the benefit of wider note circulation, and Backwell must have derived considerable value from participation in the network. At 6 per cent annually, Backwell's average daily balance of –£1,445 cost the goldsmith-banker nearly £700 in forgone interest over the eight years sampled.[23]

The system of goldsmith-banker debt clearing spans the second half of the seventeenth century. While this paper only considers quantitative evidence from 1663

---

[19] Clark, 'Restoration goldsmith-banking house', p. 35.

[20] Roseveare, 'Advancement of King's credit'.

[21] An undated letter from Sir Robert Vyner to Arlington reads, 'I have beene by many accidents much postpon'd soe yt ye money due to mee is soe farre off that I can not possible make it useful to mee. All Credit in London is much Shortened of late. I am attempting a way to enlarge my owne and doubt not to effect it to his Maties. advandtage as well as my owne, if I am (like ye lame dogg) but helpt over this Style.' Quoted in Roseveare, 'Advancement of King's credit' (PRO, SP29/225, Cal. State Papers, Dom, 1667–8, p. 113)

[22] W.J. Baumol, 'The transactions demand for cash: an inventory theoretic approach', *Quarterly Journal of Economics*, 66 (1952); M. Miller and D. Orr, 'A model of the demand for money by firms', *Quarterly Journal of Economics* (August 1966).

[23] Six per cent was the maximum legal interest rate under the usury laws at this time.

to 1672, the story of the system runs much longer. The system's roots lie somewhere in the years of the Protectorate (1648–1660).[24] By 1663 Edward Backwell was running a large banking business and was clearing demandable debt with a large number of fellow bankers. With the Stop of the Exchequer in 1672, a half dozen goldsmith-bankers who lent large sums to Charles II were forced to suspend payments.[25] Edward Backwell was greatly harmed by the Stop of the Exchequer, and his suspension of clearing activities was apparent with the cessation of his inter-banker debt clearing activities in early 1672 (see Figs. 26 and 27).

Many goldsmith-bankers, however, were not major lenders to the Crown and did not suffer ruin in 1672. Five years after the Stop, forty-four goldsmith-bankers were listed as keeping running cashes in the *Little London Directory* (1677). Charles Duncombe, Backwell's apprentice turned heir to the business, in partnership with revenue agent Richard Kent, was thriving. In the 1670s and 1680s, the ledgers of Francis Child show that he was clearing debt with prominent Fleet Street goldsmith-bankers like Thomas Fowle and Lombard Street bankers such as Charles Duncombe and Stephen Evance.[26] Despite the plague in 1665, the Great Fire in 1666, the Dutch fleet marauding the Thames in 1667, the Stop of the Exchequer in 1672 and a severe panic in 1682, the system of goldsmith-bankers continued functioning through the foundation of the Bank of England in 1694 and the turn of the eighteenth century.

II Co-ordination: The 'Gold' Boys Network

The goldsmith-bankers appear not to have had a formal institutional structure for debt clearing. Rather, an informal network of long-run relationships accepted and cleared off-setting debts. The informal system, however, did have a formal backbone — the Goldsmiths' Company. As one of the oldest and wealthiest of London's great livery companies, the Goldsmiths' Company was entrusted with guaranteeing the purity of worked precious metals. The goldsmith-bankers formed a powerful yet informal sub-set of the larger company.

The goldsmith-bankers used the Goldsmiths' Company's formal system of apprenticeship to train new bankers. Throughout London's trades, 'seven years' "genteel servitude" remained the commonest introduction to the world of business.'[27] In exchange for seven years of non-wage skilled labour and often an initial fee, the master taught the apprentice the necessary banking skills, introduced him to established bankers and developed the ground work for a long professional relationship.[28] Generations of such apprentices turned banker under the same master produced networks of goldsmith-bankers related by apprenticeship. Family trees of who was apprenticed to whom emerged.

---

[24] For example, the first extant Backwell ledger is labelled letter "I" and begins in January 1663. If each of the earlier ledgers covered a year, then Backwell's first bank ledger began in 1655.
[25] Richards, 'Stop of the Exchequer'; Horsefield '"Stop of the Exchequer" revisited'.
[26] Mitchell, 'Mr Fowle'.
[27] P. Earle, *The Making of the English Middle Class* (London, Methuen, 1989), p. 86.
[28] Many apprentices appear never to have made it to become freemen of the City much less bankers. (Goldsmiths' Company Records, Goldsmiths' Hall, London.)

GOLDSMITHS, SILVERSMITHS AND BANKERS

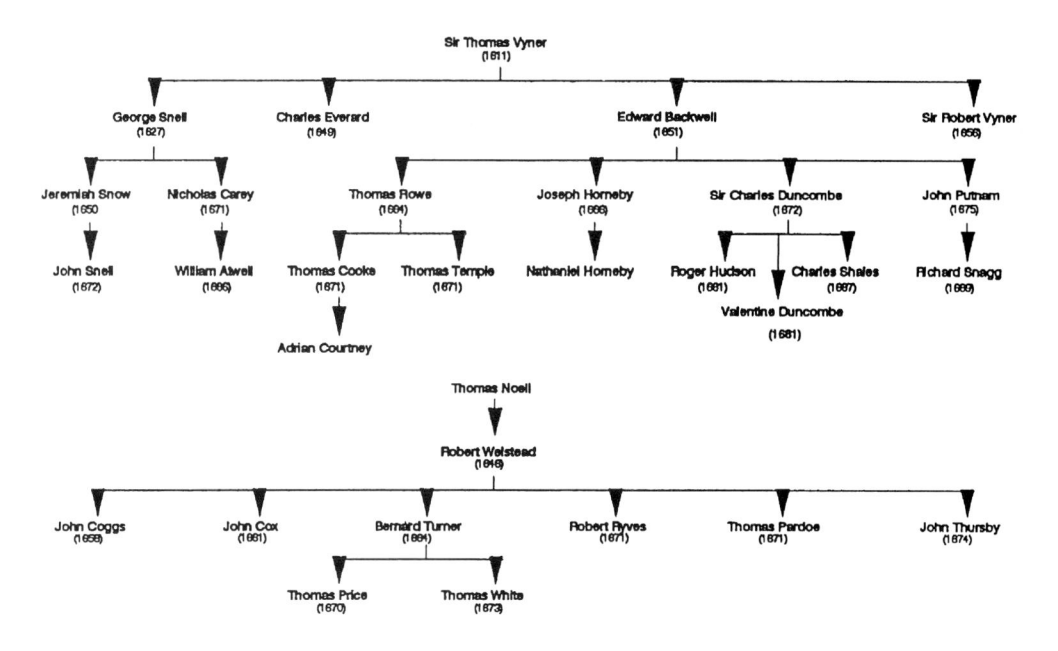

Fig. 28. The 'Gold' Boys Network: apprentices turned bankers (year of freedom)

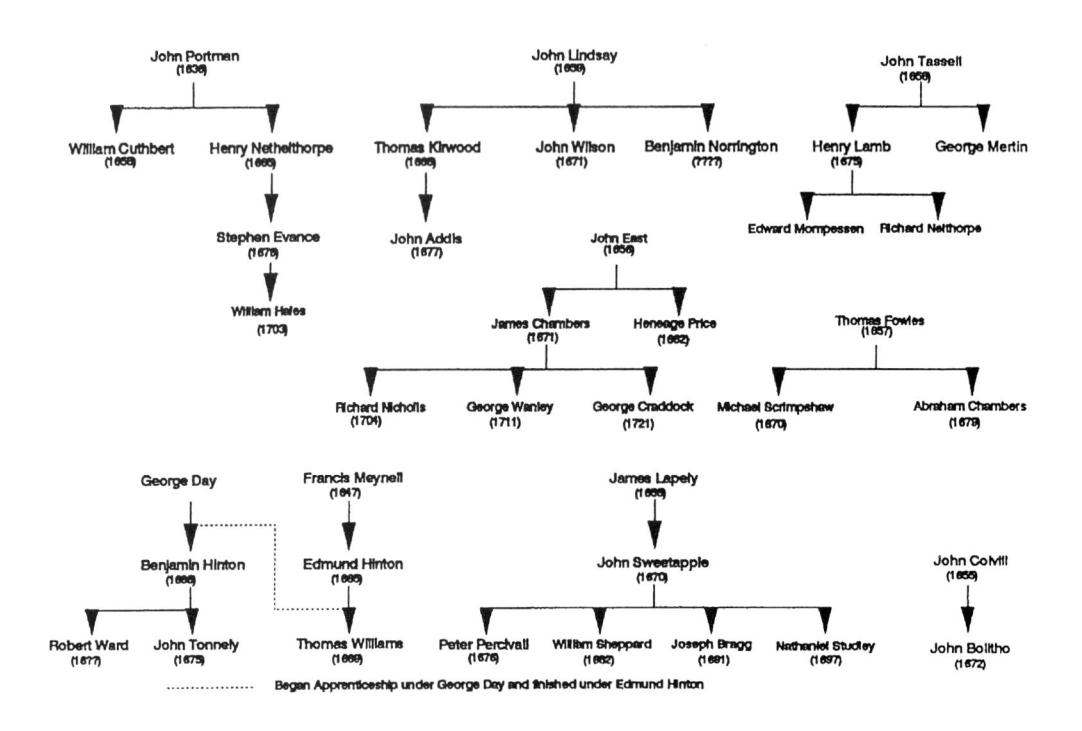

Fig. 29. 'Gold' Boys Network: additional relationships

TABLE 3

Apprentices turned bankers clearing with Edward Backwell

Apprentice	Master	Date of Freedom	Date of first clearing entry with Backwell
Thomas Cooke	Thomas Row	19 January 1671	11 May 1671
Benjamin Hinton	George Day	29 June 1666	15 November 1667
Joseph Horneby	Edward Backwell	6 July 1666	20 August 1666
Thomas Kirwood	John Lindsay	4 October 1668	7 January 1669
Thomas Pardo	Robert Welstead	17 May 1671	8 April 1671
Thomas Row	Edward Backwell	15 July 1664	18 April 1664
Robert Ryves	Robert Welstead	16 August 1671	1 September 1671
Bernard Turner	Robert Welstead	8 October 1664	15 February 1665
Thomas Williams	Edmund Hinton	29 September 1669	3 February 1670

Sources: Goldsmiths' Company Records, Goldsmiths' Hall, London; Royal Bank of Scotland Archives, London: Backwell's Ledgers EB/1–9.

Fig. 28 demonstrates how the earliest bankers like Sir Thomas Vyner and Robert Welstead produced numerous banking offspring by apprenticeship. Moreover, successful apprentices like Edward Backwell in turn produced more goldsmith-bankers. For example, a chain of great financiers to the English government ran from Sir Thomas Vyner under Cromwell through Alderman Edward Backwell under Charles II to Sir Charles Duncombe under William III. The extended families of goldsmith-bankers continued into the eighteenth century. Fig. 29 adds additional apprentice relationships between generations of goldsmith-bankers.

Not all goldsmith-bankers came up through the London apprentice system, however. Some, like Richard Kent and George Middleton, are not listed in the Goldsmiths' Company records. Middleton arrived from Scotland while Kent worked under Sir Stephen Fox, a financier and Paymaster of the Forces.[29] The system of apprenticeship, however, provided a skeleton of relationships for a network of inter-banker clearing.

During the years covered by Backwell's ledgers, a number of apprentices gained their freedom and set up independent shops. Backwell began clearing accounts with them soon after, and sometimes even before their date of freedom. Table 3 lists goldsmith-bankers who gained their freedom of the City of London and began clearing with Backwell during the years covered by his ledgers. Included in the table is Thomas Cooke who ended his apprenticeship in 1671 under Thomas Row who had himself been apprenticed to Edward Backwell, and had become free in 1664.

Apprenticeship allowed the master and the other bankers time and proximity to judge a newcomer. The relationships built during apprenticeships were important because no explicit custom or legal statement is known that delineated who was in or not in the system. Being a system of inter-banker clearing and not a clearing house, the arrangements between each banker were different and personal relationships became important. Each banker faced no known restrictions in tailoring his exposure to other bankers.

[29] C. Clay, *Public Finance and Private Wealth, the Career of Sir Stephen Fox, 1627–1716* (Oxford, 1978).

Moreover, the network of clearing may have been systems within a system. For example, Backwell cleared extensively with his fellow apprentices of Sir Thomas Vyner (George Snell and Sir Robert Vyner) and the second generation of Vyner apprentices (Jeremiah Snow, Thomas Row and Joseph Horneby) but much less so with those of Robert Welstead and his apprentices Bernard Turner, Robert Ryves and Thomas Pardo.

Undoubtedly, apprenticeship generated information and loyalties that supported greater ties and risks. The quantitative sources from only one banker's records, however, will not separate the effects of apprenticeship relations from volume of business in determining the extent of clearing.

III Control: Accounting and Clearing

Even after screening most members in the clearing network through a process of apprenticeship, every interest free overdraft Backwell accepted placed the goldsmith-banker at risk. Backwell had to balance the benefit of his overdraft privileges with the other goldsmith-bankers against not only the cost of providing interest free overdrafts but also the risk of abuse by other bankers. Backwell's colleagues could default. Moreover, bankers could attempt kiting schemes that paid one overdraft with another from a new banker. Backwell and the other goldsmith-bankers, if we accept Backwell as representative, curtailed their exposure to abuse by monitoring balances, clearing overdrafts promptly and limiting overdraft creation to third parties.

Requiring positive balances before accepting notes would not lessen the risk faced by members of London's dispersed clearing system. Other goldsmith-bankers' notes were presented to Backwell by third parties, so the issuing bankers would not know which other banker might have accepted their notes or when. Relative to a pooled, clearing-house system, uncertainty as to where notes might appear would require each banker to maintain high levels of non-interest bearing deposits with each of the other member bankers. This considerable burden could have been recompensed if the other goldsmith-bankers provided similar deposits, but reciprocal deposits would destroy the insurance that positive balances offered. If a goldsmith-banker defaulted on his notes held by Backwell, then that same banker would surely also fail to repay Backwell's security deposit. If reciprocal deposits offered no additional security but moving and assaying specie was expensive, offsetting deposits would not have been desirable.

Interest-free overdrafts would also discourage note wars among members. The cost of building up a war chest of a competitor's notes would discourage predatory runs by other bankers. Moreover, even with covering deposits, balances would occasionally prove insufficient, given that bankers could not maintain assured protective balances with all potential goldsmith-bankers. When faced with insufficient funds, the accepting banker would either have to refuse to accept the note or allow an overdraft. From the public's perspective, a seemingly random inability to deposit a note with a network member would damage the system's credibility. A system with limited members and potential weapons such as ostracism might seek to discourage non-acceptance that diminished the positive externality the network created.

If overdrafts were allowed, should interest have been charged? The goldsmith-banker holding interest-bearing negative balances had different incentives than when the same banker held interest-free overdrafts. As noted above, a banker would desire promptly to eliminate negative balances when those balances offered no return. With interest, however, the possibility of default contributed to determining tolerable overdraft amounts and durations from the perspective of the banker holding the negative balances. If the probability of default was a function of total note issue, an information problem arose. Under the no interest rate system, each banker could count on the others to police the negative balances they held. With positive interest rates, this assurance was gone. Every banker had a personal benefit in retaining interest earning balances, but every such banker also gained if all the other bankers kept overdraft balances to a minimum.

Interest charges would diminish the incentive-compatible monitoring that the no interest rate scheme enjoyed.[30] The expectation that other bankers held more of Backwell's overdrafts at interest than he held of theirs might prompt the banker to clear balances, but Backwell would have to search to discover who had large quantities of his debt. Bankers were the least cost observers of balances at their own shop, but a positive return on clearing accounts might encourage bankers not to act on this information. If bankers were in no hurry to settle the accounts of others with large overdrafts, yet bankers wanted to reduce their expensive overdrafts with others, the system-wide cost of processing information would increase exponentially as each banker would have to visit Backwell, and each other, to find out what they owed.

By not allowing his fellow bankers to personally create overdrafts, Backwell greatly reduced the potential effectiveness of kiting. Paying off one banker's overdraft with new credit from another banker required creating the new overdraft on command. Backwell did not allow his fellow bankers to present their own notes in creating overdrafts. Rather, the goldsmith-banker only accepted his fellow banker's notes from third parties. A network member trying to play an overdraft float between bankers would be unsure as which banker was receiving his notes or how much those notes might be. A scheming note issuer might circumvent this constraint by bringing third parties into the operation, but the effort needed to kite successfully would increase.

Accounting

Monitoring balances through careful, timely accounting aided Backwell's control over network overdrafts. Backwell had a system of accounting as an institutional framework that informed the network members of their balances. Information was not cost free. Many models of inventory control assume that acquiring knowledge of account balances to be effortless;[31] however, in the seventeenth century, information costs were a real constraint.

The quicker, more accurately and cheaply bankers could stay informed of balances, the better they could control their running debts. Faster attention could be given to very large balances and average balances could be reduced. In contrast, a diminished risk of dangerously large overdrafts also allowed goldsmith-bankers to tolerate larger average

---

[30] The actual loss of monitoring would allow more high risk behaviour to occur. Raising interest rates to compensate for the diminished security could exacerbate the situation. Increasing the price of note issuance would discourage low risk, low return banking and leave the higher risk, higher return bankers without addressing the monitoring problem.

[31] Miller and Orr, 'Model of demand for money'.

deficits, but the effect of quicker information on average balances is uncertain. The variance of balances, however, would clearly fall as bankers could swiftly address uncomfortably large balances.

During the years covered by the ledgers of Edward Backwell, the goldsmith-banker altered his system of accounting towards improved monitoring. In his ledgers, Backwell switched from a system of independent to a system of connected double entry accounting. Throughout his ledgers, Backwell added each folio's credits and debits separately to balance each account. The innovation meant Backwell began pairing each transaction with a specific off-setting entry. Before 1666, Backwell did not record entries as balancing a particular pre-existing entry.

The practical effect of knowing on the spot which entries had been cleared was a quicker knowledge of balances still outstanding. Without connected entries, the entirety of the debits and credits since the last totalling had to be added and the difference found to know that account balance at that moment. With precise write-offs, only those debits or credits not yet cleared needed to be summed, so transaction costs were saved and balances made easier to ascertain.

An example from the accounts of Thomas Row will assist. Table 4 presents the goldsmith-banker Thomas Row's clearing account with Backwell for March 1664/5 and January 1665/6. The ledger (Ledger N) covering the nine months in between is not extant. In March 1665, the descriptions of debit and credit entries make no mention of any off-setting transaction. Debits (on the left) are paid out by Backwell to Row ('him' entries) or others such as Robert Blanchard, a goldsmith-banker, and Morris & Clayton, a partnership of money-scriveners. On the right side, Row's account is credited for money and notes deposited by Row and other individuals such as fellow goldsmith-bankers, Sir Thomas Vyner and Sir Francis Meynell. The credit and debit transactions bear no immediate relationship with each other.

By January 1666, the system of accounting had changed.[32] Virtually every entry now had a precise off-setting transaction. On both the debit and credit sides, many entries were

---

[32] The diffusion of the accounting innovation was complete across all of Backwell's accounts in Ledger 'O' (1666). Thomas Row, the goldsmith-banker in Table 4, had been Backwell's apprentice, so the new accounting was not functioning within Backwell's closest circle before the general change over. Over the life of the missing Ledger 'N' (25 March 1665 to 31 December 1665), the switch occurred. Where innovation came from, and why the innovation was adopted when it was remain unclear. The London goldsmith-bankers were familiar with Continental systems of exchange bank accounting and may have changed the approach from simultaneous, inter-account recording to lagged, intra-account bookkeeping. The timing of the innovation coincided with a very hectic period for Backwell. While out of the kingdom on Charles II's business in 1665, Backwell suffered a run that required the Crown to pronounce full backing of the tallies and treasury orders held by Backwell (see Clark, 'Backwell as Royal Agent'). The switch also paralleled the introduction of a new hand to the ledgers, likely Charles Duncombe. The beginning of the new handwriting corresponds with the year of Duncombe's entering his apprenticeship with Backwell and matches the handwriting on the back of a note written by Backwell to Duncombe held today by the Royal Bank of Scotland. Duncombe's arrival came soon after the loss of Backwell's cashier Robert Shaw who died in the plague that swept London in 1665 (see Clark, 'Restoration banking-house'). The shocks of 1665 may have created a break in the natural order of business that allowed Backwell an opportunity to adjust his banking practices. The events of 1665, especially the untimely loss of his cashier, may also have jarred Backwell into instituting an accounting regime allowing for easier monitoring of his own staff.

TABLE 4

Account of Thomas Row at Edward Backwell's shop

March 1664/5									
Day	Debits	£	s	d	Day	Credits	£	s	d
1	Wm Horne	1000			6	Johna Dawes, which was recd at Dan Edwards	100		
3	Ball	200			7	mony	707		
8	Hugh Mason ordered the 13th day of Feb	86			9	Wynne	30		
8	Morris & Claiton	96	12	6	9	Mild gold at 15d, 60	63	15	
9	him old gold	71	6	8	10	R Holder	76	6	4
16	so much Joseph pd his man yesterday	100			11	Hen Ballow	100		
17	Blanchard	50			15	mild gold 50, 7	60	11	3
17	him p contant	500			16	mild gold 250 at 15d	265	12	6
18	Dunkin	160			16	severall	666	10	4
20	him p Contant	600			17	milled gold at 15d, 20	21	5	
20	him p Contant	300			18	mild gold, at 15d, 15	15	18	9
17	Nic Warren	29	7	11	20	three notes rec of him	499	18	
16	one salver & cup 74oz at 5s 10d	21	11	8	20	T Vyner	273	15	
22	lent old gold 350	350			21	mild gold, 191 at 15d	20	3	9
23	him p contant	500			21	Ball orderd 10th Feb	370	10	
23	wm Prickman	130			21	Finch ordered 23 Feb	100		
24	content p Robt Porter	500			24	Meynell	400		
					24	Savage	400		

January 1666									
Day	Debits	£	s	d	Day	Credits	£	s	d
1	20 milled gold at 20d p Tho Temple	21	13	4	1	note	110	16	1
4	his man	100			1	note	100		
4	his man	110	16	1	4	note	450		
4	Boone	300			5	y 4th	300		
5	y 4th	450			5	note	118	15	
9	Corcellis	60			10	money	500		
10	DiBusty	254	14		10	money	300		
10	Sr John Fredericke	200			13	Adrian & Manrois 200, Bathurst 200	275	14	7
11	Snow	400			15	y 15th	275	14	7
12	Dulivier	223	8	9	15	y 10	454	14	
12	Freeman	160			15	y 12	160		
12	Frohocke	44			15	y 12	165	3	9
12	Dulivier	165	3	9	15	y 12	223	8	9
15	Dunkin	275	14	7	15	y 4	60		
15	y 5th	118	15		15	y 12	44		
15	y £800	400			15	Conguard	50		
15	Adrian 200, Bathurst 200	400			17	y 10	100		
16	Wm Batteshay	100			19	Lawr DiBusty	588	4	5
18	Coguards	50			20	mild gold 300 at 19d	323	15	
18	Dibusty	588	4	5	23	Conyers	100		
22	Conyers	100			26	Wade	100		
24	mild gold	323	15		24	small cup		18	6
26	Wade	100			29	y 27th	251	3	4
27	Dibustry	251	3	4					

described solely in reference to earlier transactions. On 5 January, Row was debited for £450 with the description 'y 4th'. The description refers to a note for £450 that Row had credited to his account one day earlier. Row was withdrawing funds to balance a specific credit. The same occurred on the credit side. On 5 January, the ledger described Row's credit of £300 as 'y 4th'. Row was clearing his account with Backwell with regards to the specific debit of £300 that Backwell paid to Mr. Boone from Row's account. Even the credits with named descriptions exactly match debits such as with Conguard on 15 January, DiBusty on 19 January, Conyers on 23 January.

The change in accounting produced very precise folio balances. Under the earlier regime, the difference between credits and debits at the end of a folio would be transferred to the top of the next folio for the continued life of the account in question. With the change to connected entries, these residuals all but disappear. After the switch, most folios end in perfect balance: not one pence difference between debits and credits.

The major benefit to Backwell and his customers of the new connected entries system was not a cleaner ledger. The ledger was a final record rather than work in progress. The change in the final ledgers revealed that a significant adjustment in the point of transaction accounting did occur between March 1665 and January 1666. While it is unknown how the exact process of recording transactions worked, Backwell did begin pairing offsetting payments at the front desk. The change in accounting procedures reduced the average and the variance of the aggregate balances held by Backwell. From March 1663 to March 1665, Backwell shouldered an average overdraft £1,037 larger than after 1666. The standard deviation also fell from £5,792 to £4,311. Importantly, the total pound volume of transactions increased in the later period. Measuring debit transactions only, the average daily debit rose from £1,208 to £1,642, so the fall in daily average and variance was not driven by less business.

The character of Backwell's clearing activities became relatively more tolerant of initial overdrafts but more expeditious in reducing ongoing negative balances with the innovation in accounting. The improved flow of information allowed Backwell to reduce overdrafts quickly which lowered the average balance and the overall variance, despite a larger flow of clearing. Nevertheless, the new accounting regime allowed for more variance *relative* to average balances. The coefficient of variation, the standard deviation divided by the absolute value of the mean, rose from 2.57 before 1666 to 3.55 afterwards. The rising coefficient of variation indicates that the mean fell faster than the variance. With his improved information, Backwell was not restricting initial overdrafts. Rather, the goldsmith-banker was tolerating even larger overdrafts. Backwell accepted larger initial overdrafts because he could now control his overdraft exposure more effectively than before.

Clearing

Beyond monitoring his exposure to fellow bankers, Backwell actively cleared overdrafts on a daily basis. Backwell's post-1666 accounting system enables calculation of when clearing debits were created and when they were cleared. Again, this information exists because Backwell went to the trouble to collect and maintain these records. By his own efforts, the goldsmith-banker revealed that he valued timely knowledge of when debits were created and retired.

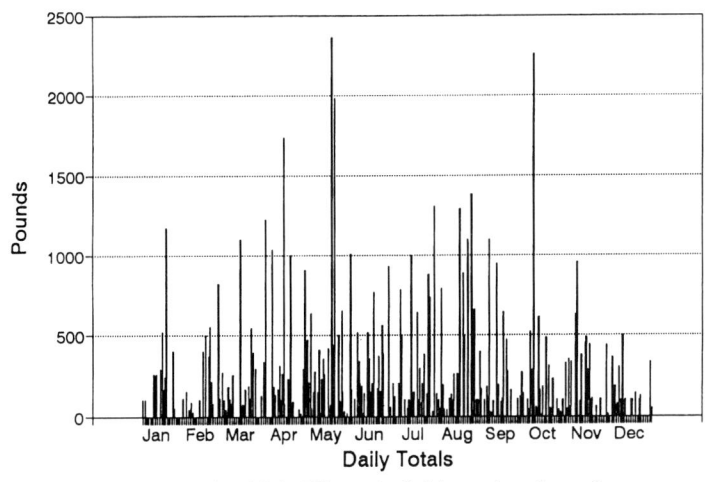

Fig. 30A. Hinton's debits to be cleared

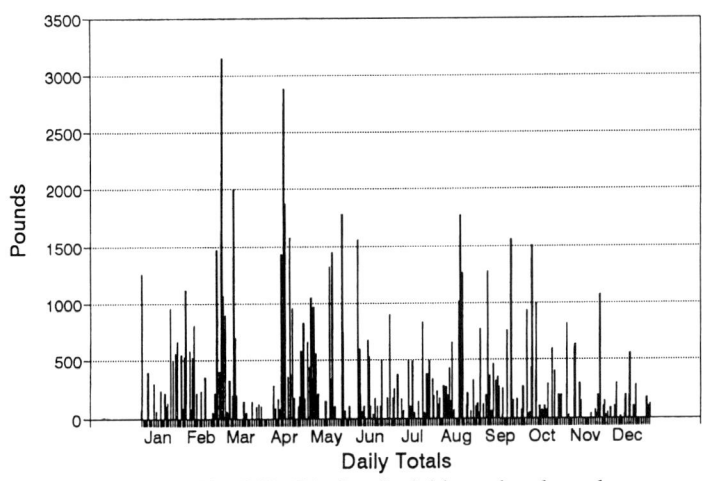

Fig. 30B. Lindsay's debits to be cleared

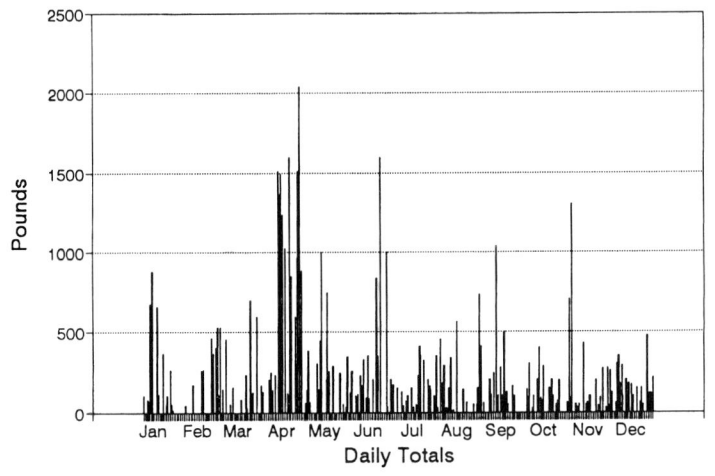

Fig. 30C. Row's debits to be cleared

This section considers the clearing accounts of three goldsmith-bankers on a detailed level for the year 1670. Thomas Row, John Lindsay and Benjamin Hinton have been selected because all three operated on Lombard Street with Backwell and all three had clearing activities of similar sizes. Fig. 30 A–C report the daily pound value of debits on Hinton, Lindsay and Row respectively that Backwell recorded as needing to be cleared in 1670. Table 5 below, provides the summary statistics for each banker's distribution of individual debits to be cleared (Figs. 30 A–C) with Backwell in 1670. Although Benjamin Hinton had fifty per cent more debits requiring clearing than Thomas Row did, all three bankers had similar flows of notes by the public into Backwell. All had identical medians and modes of £100 except for Lindsay's median of £116.

TABLE 5

Characteristics of debits with Backwell to be cleared, by banker in 1670

	Benjamin Hinton	John Lindsay	Thomas Row
Mean	£161	£229	£173
Median	£100	£116	£100
Mode (No. of occurrences,	£100	£100	£100
% of total observations)	(64, 14%)	(48, 13%)	(33, 10%)
Standard Deviation	£217	£317	£201
Minimum	£5.40	£9.95	£6.75
Maximum	£2,000	£2,911	£1,447
Number of observations	457	380	324

The three bankers, however, had different backgrounds. Thomas Row had been Backwell's apprentice until gaining his freedom in 1664 (see Table 3). Row provides a proxy for the relationship between close bankers. Row and Backwell had close business dealings including the loan of £30,000 from Row to Backwell in August 1670. John Lindsay was free of the City in 1658 and had regular dealings with Backwell over the life of Backwell's extant ledgers. Lindsay represents an older, proven, long-run business colleague. Benjamin Hinton ended his apprenticeship in 1666, but he did not begin clearing activity with Backwell until late in 1667. Given the fire in 1666 and the runs on Lombard Street in 1667, Hinton's delay seems warranted. Hinton represents the status of newcomers to the network.

The three goldsmith-bankers also differed in their overall balances with Backwell. Figs. 31 A–C present Hinton's, Lindsay's and Row's total daily balance with Backwell over 1670. Both Lindsay and Hinton usually had negative balances while Row's balance was usually positive. Hinton's and Lindsay's daily balances also had higher variances than Row's account had. Fig. 32 adds a graph of the daily balance of all goldsmith-bankers with Backwell over the year 1670. Backwell's total exposure to his fellow goldsmiths fell considerably after the summer of 1670. The dramatic flip in goldsmith-bankers' overall balance was caused by two notes presented by George Snell to Backwell on 13 June 1670, for £6,000 payable on 13 July and £5,500 payable

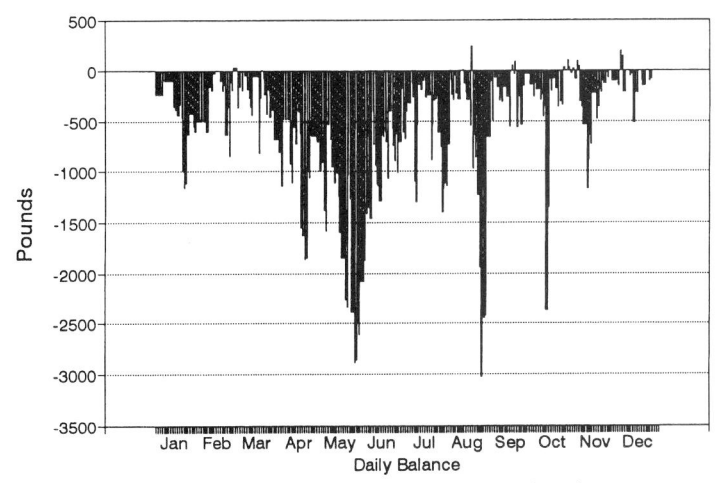

Fig. 31A. Balance of Benjamin Hinton

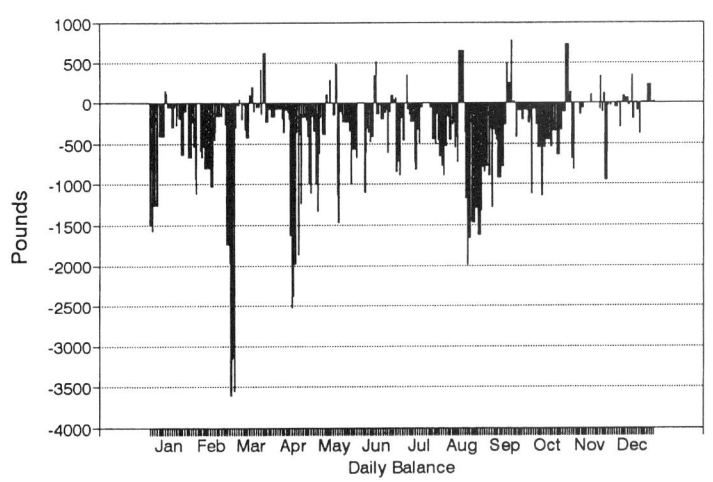

Fig. 31B. Balance of John Lindsay

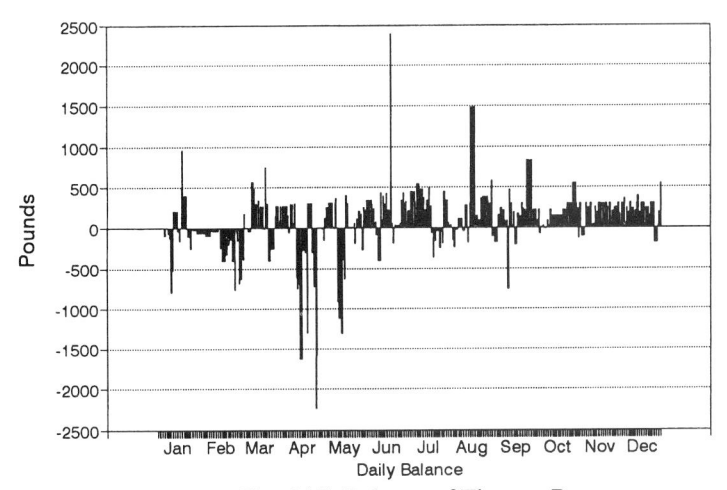

Fig. 31C. Balance of Thomas Row

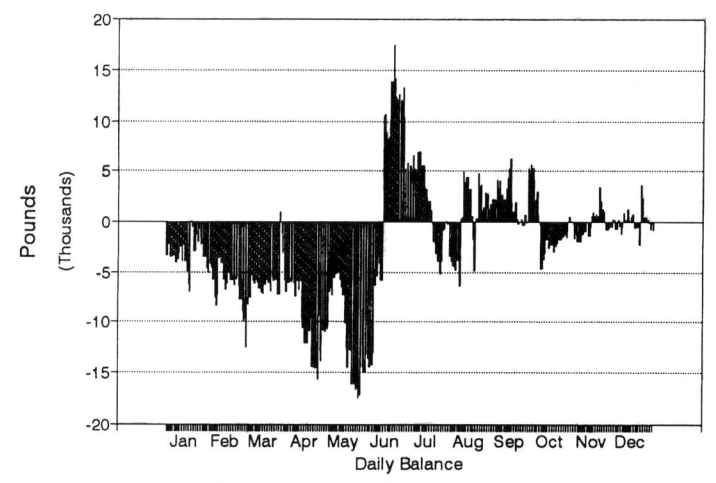

Fig. 32. Balance of all goldsmith-bankers.

TABLE 6

Characteristics of banker balances with Backwell in 1670

	Benjamin Hinton	John Lindsay	Thomas Row	All bankers
Mean	–£543	–£370	£90	–£2,452
Median	–£354	–£190	£152	–£2,126
Standard Deviation	£607	£591	£407	£6,048
Minimum	–£3,026	–£3,611	–£2,243	–£17,480
Maximum	£238	£784	£2,402	£17,476

on 13 August of that year.[33] Table 6 reports the summary statistics for the goldsmith-bankers' balances.

Given that all three bankers had very similar flow of debits into Backwell, the considerable difference between Hinton's and Lindsay's negative balances on the one hand and Row's positive balances on the other must stem from the credit side of their accounts with Backwell. Thomas Row presented to Backwell many more notes for credits than did the other two goldsmith-bankers sampled. The initiating credits summarised in Table 7 below, are entries that Backwell recorded as himself owing the other bankers. These credits were then later (Figs. 31 A–C, 32) cleared by an explicit debit. The calculations in Table 7 exclude nearly £42,000 in bullion that Row was credited with from 20 August 1670 until finally being completely repaid by the East India Company in January 1671.

The larger inflow of Backwell's notes from Row, relative to Hinton or Lindsay, suggests Row retained more of Backwell's notes, net of clearing, than the other two

---

[33] The £6,000 was duly paid by Backwell on 13 July 1670. The £5,500 was paid off in instalments of £1,000, £1,801. 15s. 9d., £1,000 and £1,098. 4s.3d. on 13, 15, 17 and 19 August respectively. On 13 July, Snell was credited for an additional £5,000 that was cleared over the following week.

TABLE 7
Characteristics of credits with Backwell to be cleared, by banker in 1670

	Benjamin Hinton	John Lindsay	Thomas Row
Mean	£136	£257	£301
Median	£100	£140	£163
Mode (#, % of N)	£50, £100 (5, 11%)	£100 (4, 8%)	£200 (3, 4%)
Standard Deviation	£146	£305	£440
Minimum	£10.7	£31	£20
Maximum	£730	£1,300	£3,011
Number of observations	45	48	71

goldsmith-bankers. When time came to clear, if Backwell did not have an offsetting note of Row's, Thomas Row was likely credited by Backwell for the surplus Backwell notes that Row held. Row's consistently positive balances would be explained if Row was routinely presenting Backwell with more notes than vice versa. Lindsay's and Hinton's consistently negative balances might be explained by the reverse situation: Backwell was receiving more of their notes (Table 5) from the public then they were receiving of his notes. Unfortunately, as the other bankers' ledgers have not survived, the hypothesis cannot be verified.

The same accounting system that permitted the separate examination of debits (goldsmith-banker notes) presented to Backwell by the public, and credits (Backwell's notes) presented to Backwell by account holding bankers, also allows the calculation of how long entries took to be cleared. An examination of the rate of clearing of the three bankers' debits presented in Figs. 30 A–C reveals prompt clearing occurred. Table 8 reports the days each debit took to clear. The days to clearing include Sundays, so these figures overstate clearing times for days greater than zero (the same day). Moreover, the bias increases with the span of time until clearing. A majority of notes are cleared after one or two days and over ninety per cent are cleared within one week. Inter-banker debt clearing was a recurrent, short run affair.

TABLE 8
Days to clear banker debits

	Benjamin Hinton			John Lindsay			Thomas Row		
Days to clear	Debits	per cent	Cum %	Debits	per cent	Cum%	Debits	per cent	Cum%
0 to <1	86	19%	19%	110	29%	29%	96	30%	30%
1 to <2	122	27%	46%	107	28%	57%	86	27%	56%
2 to <3	96	21%	67%	72	19%	76%	57	18%	74%
3 to <4	55	12%	79%	35	9%	85%	40	12%	86%
4 to <5	27	6%	84%	19	5%	90%	12	4%	90%
5 to <6	17	4%	88%	14	4%	94%	12	4%	94%
6 to <7	15	3%	91%	4	1%	95%	9	3%	96%
7 to <8	16	4%	95%	9	2%	97%	2	1%	97%
8 and above	23	5%	100%	10	3%	100%	10	3%	100%
Total	457			380			324		

0 = Same Day. Days to clearing includes Sundays

Thomas Row and John Lindsay are striking in Table 5 for their similarity. Moreover, both were routinely clearing faster than Benjamin Hinton. In two days, Lindsay and Row each averaged the clearing of three quarters of their respective notes. Hinton managed only two-thirds over the same period. The former pair of bankers both broke ninety per cent clearing in less than five days while Hinton took two additional days.

The similarity of Lindsay with Row is curious, given that Lindsay's stream of debits and overall balance were comparable to Hinton's, rather than Row's debits and balances. Row and Lindsay did share longer and closer business relationships with Backwell than Hinton. Why increased familiarity would translate into quicker clearing, if it did at all, requires consideration of what might be determining the actual timing of clearing. Unfortunately, there is no contemporary qualitative description as to how the actual process of clearing worked. The simplest story would be that bankers cleared on regular days of the week. This possibility will be tested below.

A more complicated story might be that clearing occurred whenever either banker made the effort. One could propose a framework for characterising the clearing process by assuming firstly that each banker accepted the other bankers' notes from the general public at par; and secondly that each banker could demand clearance at any time. A trade-off emerges. Each banker weighs the benefit of clearing the other banker's debt he is holding against the expected amount of his own debt held by the other banker. For example, Backwell initiates clearing with Benjamin Hinton when, **$Debits_t(1+i)$ > $E[Notes_t](1+i)$**. Debits are the pound value of Hinton's notes held by Backwell at time **t**. **E[Notes]** are the expected pound value of Backwell's notes held by Hinton at time **t**. Backwell will not know the true level of his notes held by Hinton until actual clearing. The interest rate is represented by **i** and assumes both bankers have equally good uses for the money. If Backwell thinks he holds more of Hinton's notes than Hinton does of his, Backwell will push to clear the accounts. Hinton has the reverse incentive. The quality of expectations would benefit from the highly repetitive nature of London's clearing system.

The implication of this two-party clearing system is that the nature of Backwell's relationship with each goldsmith banker should differ depending on whether Backwell usually initiates clearing or responds. If Backwell is initiating clearing, the number of days until clearing should fall as Backwell receives more of the other Banker's notes. Backwell will be more likely to demand payment as larger amounts of the other banker's debt accumulates with Backwell. Backwell will respond to large debits on day **t** and new debits on following days by speeding up the clearing process. In contrast, if Backwell is often responding to another banker's clearing initiative, the expectations of the other banker drives the timing of the clearing process. The timing of clearing would not be responsive to when debits arrive into Backwell's shop from the public or to the pound value of those notes. The other banker, say Thomas Row, would be responding to the inflow of Backwell's notes at Row's shop. The information in Backwell's ledgers would not carry predictive power.

Backwell would be most likely to initiate clearing with goldsmith-bankers that were running large deficits. Backwell would be forced to clear by other bankers if they expected to have more of Backwell's notes than he had of theirs. If the other banker's expectations were correct, the initiating banker should have had low debit levels with

Backwell relative to Backwell's debit levels with the initiating banker. Although the other bankers' ledgers are not extant, Thomas Row's positive balances with Backwell suggests that Row accumulated more of Backwell's notes than Backwell did of Row's notes. Thomas Row was a potential initiator of clearing with Backwell and possibly in contrast to Hinton and Lindsay.

IV The Nature of Banking in London

The nature of the clearing accounts in Backwell's ledgers was markedly different from Continental exchange banks. Goldsmith-banking was dominated by transactions between customer and *banker* and not transactions between customer and counter party *facilitated by a banker*. Unlike exchange banks, London's goldsmith-bankers were constantly acting as credit-creating counter parties. Credit creation allowed for note issuance and fractional reserve banking. The introduction of bank credit by London's goldsmith-bankers marked a fundamental break from traditional exchange banking.

The difference in accounting reveals the essential differences in the actual process of debt clearing between London and Amsterdam. Entries in the ledgers of Amsterdam's Wisselbank (Exchange Bank) always listed a corresponding counter party other than the bank. This was because the Wisselbank only honoured orders to pay backed by positive balances.[34] In turn, the Wisselbank's system of accounting listed the offsetting counter party in the description of all transactions.[35] Although fully aware of how the Wisselbank handled its affairs, London's goldsmith-bankers cleared debts without regular cross referencing (referral to an offsetting counter party account). Instead of clearing between accounts, Backwell himself became a principal. The goldsmith-banker assumed the offsetting debits and then later cleared the transaction. By stepping into the clearing process as a counter party, Backwell created credit.

The differences recur when dealing with how the intermediaries accounted for themselves. To keep its system of accounting consistent, the Wisselbank listed itself as a counter party. When a customer deposited/withdrew money at the Wisselbank, the Exchange Bank's strong room was debited/credited.[36] Backwell did create personal accounts for his household expenses and bullion transactions, but no explicit account is kept of Backwell's as a counter party relative to his customers. Instead, Backwell's position is the omnipresent but unstated mirror image of his ledgers.

London's bankers did not maintain an explicit account for themselves as counter parties because they performed a different type of banking than found at the Wisselbank. The foremost examples of this change were bank notes. The Wisselbank did not operate with bank notes (promises to pay), only orders. The creation of short-run debt accompanying the widespread use of bank notes in London meant a much higher level of banker to customer transactions than Amsterdam's pure customer to customer system. An explicit account for Backwell himself would have meant a veritable duplication of

---

[34] van der Wee, 'Monetary, credit and banking systems'; J.G. van Dillen, 'The Bank of Amsterdam', *History of the Principal Public Banks* (The Hague, 1934), pp. 79–123; W.D.H. Assar, 'Bills of Exchange and Agency in the 18th Century Law of Holland and Zeeland', in V. Piergiovanni (ed.), *Courts and the Development of commercial Law* (Berlin, 1987), pp. 103–130.
[35] Amsterdam Municipal Archives, 5077/4: Wisselbank Ledgers, Indices and Balances.
[36] Amsterdam Municipal Archives, 5077/4.

paperwork. The cost in time and material would have been substantial. The relative number of banker to customer transactions in Amsterdam were much smaller, so the logging of the Wisselbank's own account was manageable.

Moreover, a public record of the banker's balances would have exposed the extent of debt creation performed by the banker. Since the goldsmith-bankers were working with fractional reserves and varying balances, an explicit account would let depositors know when the banker was at risk.[37] In a world with monitoring depositors[38] or random withdrawals,[39] bankers would suffer more runs if the public knew when the banker was vulnerable from fractional reserves.

The economic change in the nature of the intermediary was from the clearing of positive balances (the Wisselbank did not tolerate negative balances) to the creation of short-run bank debt.[40] In the period between Backwell's paying out on behalf of an account and receiving a balancing deposit, the goldsmith-banker was floating his own credit. The system of clearing reflects a new, credit-creating type of banking occurring in London. The goldsmith-bankers issued promissory debt, worked from fractional reserves and regularly created short-run credit.

Conclusion

Edward Backwell conducted extensive clearing operations as a member of London's seventeenth-century network of goldsmith-bankers. The quantitative evidence presented in this paper demonstrates that Backwell was managing the substantial overdraft accounts of nineteen fellow bankers. With the introduction of an innovative accounting process and daily clearing, Backwell was better able to control his exposure to the interest free loans that negative balances represented. Through the co-ordination of a clearing network around a subset of the London's Goldsmiths' Company and the incentive compatible control of balances by monitoring and clearing, a resilient system of inter-banker debt clearing thrived in pre-Bank of England London.

The network of inter-banker clearing was critical to the spreading use of bank notes and cheques as means of payment. The goldsmith-bankers promoted the common use of demandable debt that the Bank of England would later take full advantage of. With the creation of demandable debt, Backwell and his fellow bankers marked a clear break with the Continental exchange banks. The goldsmith-bankers created a private banking system that became an important foundation for the Financial Revolution that started in late seventeenth-century England.

---

[37] See Quinn, 'Banking before the Bank', chapter 4.

[38] C. Calomiris and C. Kahn, 'The role of demandable debt in restructuring optimal banking arrangements', *American Economic Review*, 81 (1991), pp. 497–513; C. Calomiris, 'Regulation, industrial structure, and instability in US banking: an historical perspective', in M. Klausner and L.J. White (eds.), *Structural Change in Banking* (Homewood, Ill.: Business One Irwin, 1993).

[39] D. Diamond and P. Dybvig, 'Bank runs, liquidity and deposit insurance', *Journal of Political Economy* (June 1983), pp. 401–19.

[40] Even the Wisselbank was not fully forthright. The Amsterdam Exchange Bank listed the flow of specie in and out but did not report the stock nor specify whether transactions were in gold or silver.(Amsterdam Municipal Archives)

The interaction between English and Huguenot goldsmiths in the late seventeenth and early eighteenth centuries

EMMA PACKER

The question of how important a part foreign craftsmen played in the lives of English goldsmiths is an issue specific to the goldsmiths' trade in the late seventeenth and early eighteenth centuries. This period in the history of silver is characterised by the influx of French Huguenot craftsmen into England after the revocation of the Edict of Nantes in 1685, bringing with them the skills and techniques that they had been practising in France. Centring around the findings of an investigation into a sample group of twenty-five Orphans Court inventories for members of the Goldsmiths' Company and by taking one as a case study, this paper discusses how significant a role the Huguenots played in the lives of English goldsmiths, who were free of the Goldsmiths' Company during this period.[1]

The inventories studied date between the years 1695 and 1732. All follow the same basic format: each lists the freeman's assets — that is their household goods, details of shop goods, stocks and securities. The Orphans Court inventories are highly unusual in that they also list the freeman's debtors and creditors which enables the historian to gain a greater understanding of the individual's business dealings, in terms of who were his clients, suppliers and subcontractors. The theories expressed in this paper centre mostly around the information contained in the lists of debtors and creditors.

One particular inventory, that of Thomas Folkingham, reflects the overall findings of the Orphans Court inventories.[2] By piecing together his business career and looking at surviving objects that bear his mark, this paper builds up a picture of his suppliers and subcontractors in order to demonstrate the changing role played by Huguenot craftsmen in his career.

Thomas Folkingham was born in Thrusley, Derbyshire, the son of a clerk, around the year 1678. By 1692 he had moved to London and in that year became apprenticed to John Bache for the term of seven years. Bache is known from the Court Minutes Books at Goldsmiths' Hall to have been a working goldsmith and to have been in partnership with the goldsmith William Denny. Folkingham is recorded in Heal's *London Goldsmiths* as a working goldsmith at the Golden Ball in St. Swithin's Lane, just off Lombard Street

---

[1] Corporation of London Records Office (CLRO), Orphans Court Inventories (Orph. Inv.) Goldsmiths' Co. freemen: Robert Hill, Hector Moore, Nicholas Cary, Thomas Williams, Thomas Issod, John Johnson, John Jackson, William Goodwin, Francis Greville, Peter Floyer, Samuel Day, Christopher Canner, Michael Wilson, John Ward, Lancelot Baker, Simon Knight, James Metcalfe, John Downes, John Rusden, Thomas Ash, John Partridge, Humphrey Dell, Thomas Sadler, Thomas Folkingham, Thomas Port.

[2] CLRO, Orph. Inv. 3330a and b, Thomas Folkingham.

in the City, from 1706 to 1720.³ 1706 was the year when he registered his first mark as a largeworker and was also the year in which he took his first apprentice (Fig. 33). He entered a second mark in 1720, again giving his address as St. Swithin's Lane. However, by 1725 he had moved to the Golden Ball behind the Royal Exchange, a more salubrious address, between Threadneedle Street and Cornhill, where his business remained until he died. Folkingham died on 26 October 1729 and was buried at St. Benetfink Church, London, leaving a widow, his second wife, and three orphans. His inventory was written a month later on 24 November. During his lifetime he had built up a successful business, first as a working goldsmith and later as a large retailer. The *Political State of Great Britain* wrote, 'two days before died Mr Falkenham, a very noted goldsmith, said to have left upwards of £30,000'.⁴

It is known that after completing his apprenticeship Folkingham began his career as a working goldsmith. In 1700 Folkingham married Elizabeth Denny, the daughter of his master's partner. This was advantageous for Folkingham as he appears to have inherited his first premises from his father-in-law. As Denny is known to have been a working goldsmith, it is probable that this first establishment had a workshop.⁵

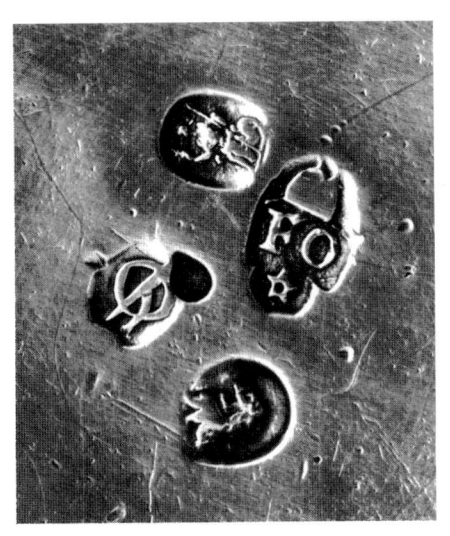

Fig. 33. Thomas Folkingham's sponsor's mark, registered in 1706.
(Birmingham Museum and Art Gallery)

However, Folkingham's inventory of 1729 gives a different impression and implies that by the end of his career he was working solely in the capacity of a retailer. The inventory lists a large amount of stock valued at £1986. 5s. 2d.; his shop goods included over fifty-three different types of plate which were valued at just over £1100. His stock also included objects of vertu, £268 worth of jewels, and gold and coins worth £170 (Fig. 34). No working tools were mentioned in the inventory, which again implies that Folkingham was not running a workshop at the time of his death. As stated above, Folkingham moved addresses between the years 1720 and 1724 and it may be that this more up-market establishment had retailing facilities only, with no space for a workshop.

If Folkingham was acting as a retailer, then it must be assumed that he was subcontracting his work out to other goldsmiths and this is confirmed in his inventory. His list of creditors in 1729 includes the names of several working goldsmiths who registered marks at Goldsmiths' Hall as largeworkers. For instance, he owed James Gould (a specialist candlestick maker based nearby in Gutter Lane) £5. 10s., and Edward Cornock (whose mark appears on a number of salvers and tobacco boxes and who again worked in Gutter Lane) 14s. 8d. Other creditors included John Clark, a largeworker

---

[3] A. Heal, *The London Goldsmiths 1200–1800* (Newton Abbot, 1972), p. 153
[4] A.G. Grimwade, *The London Goldsmiths 1697–1837* (2nd edn.; London, 1982), p. 511
[5] Denny died in 1706 and Folkingham is recorded by Heal as being at the same address from 1706 onwards.

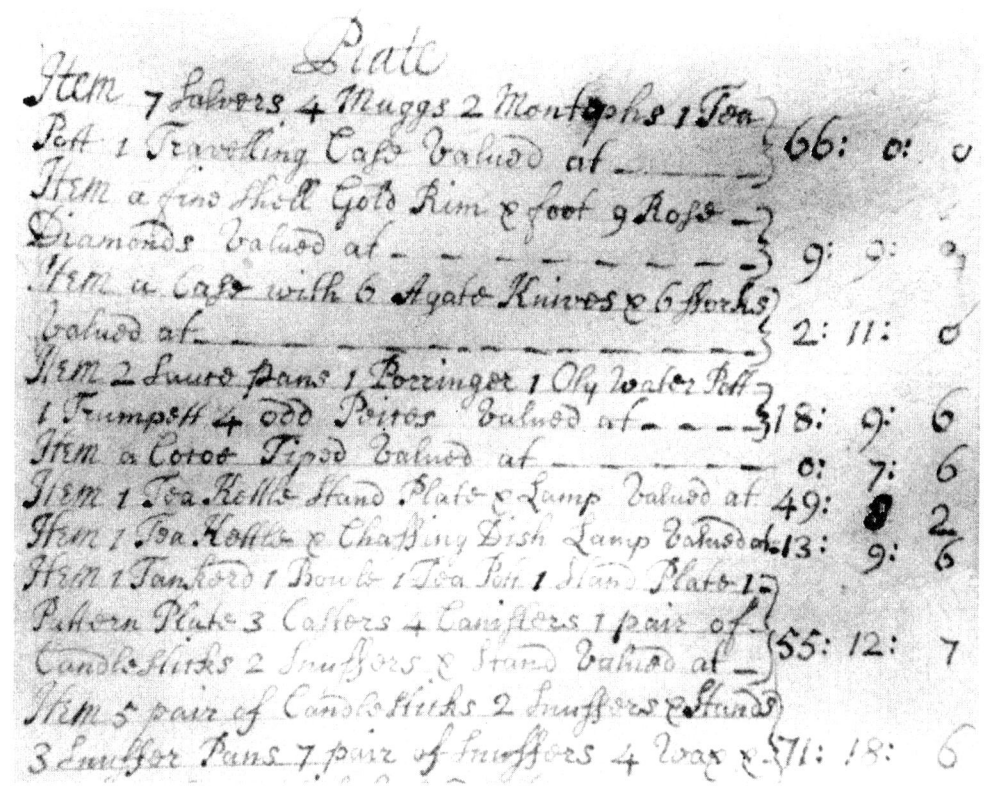

Fig. 34. Extract from the inventory of Thomas Folkingham, detailing his shop goods.
(Corporation of London Records Office)

in Foster Lane, William Toone of Cripplegate, and James Goodwin of Noble Street. Although the exact nature of the debts are unknown, these creditors may well have been acting as Folkingham's suppliers.

Folkingham's inventory therefore provides an insight into the kind of people with whom he was dealing at the time of his death in 1729. At this date, according to his inventory, his suppliers were English working goldsmiths based in the locality surrounding Goldsmiths' Hall. Importantly, Folkingham's list of debtors and creditors does not include the names of any foreign craftsmen. This is surprising when considering the surviving objects that date from between the years of 1720 and 1729 which appear to contradict the findings of his inventory.

A change in style can be seen in objects bearing Folkingham's mark from 1720 onwards. Several pieces in a distinctively French style were noted bearing Folkingham's mark and dating between these years (1720–29) and these objects stand out from the rest of his wares for the quality of their execution and design. These wares are mainly luxury items, made in the fashionable style of the time. For example, a pair of candlesticks of 1725 survive in the Regence style bearing the mark of Folkingham overstriking that of another (Fig. 35). The intricate decoration and high standard of craftsmanship implies that they were most probably made or decorated by a Huguenot. A helmet-shaped ewer of about 1720 at the Ashmolean Museum, again bearing the Folkingham mark, shows the influence of the Huguenots in its form and decoration.[6] It has a scroll handle terminating in a female mask and decorated with guilloche, diaper pattern and pendant husk motifs — all decorative features that were used widely by the Huguenot craftsmen.

Also included in this group of his objects is a casket of 1725.[7] Again the decoration on the casket, especially the chased relief panels on a matted background and the use of the lambrequin motif, appear to be the work of a foreign craftsmen. Another casket from a toilet service bearing the mark of David Willaume (himself a Huguenot) and also dated 1725 survives in the Royal Ontario Museum, Canada. This second casket is

Fig. 35. A pair of candlesticks bearing the mark of Thomas Folkingham, 1725.
(Tessiers Ltd.)

very similar in form and appears to have identical chased panels to the Folkingham example. This implies that either Folkingham was stamping Willaume's work with his own sponsor's mark or both of them were obtaining work from the same outworker and marking it as their own.[8]

The style imported from the French court and characteristic of the Huguenots' work was very much in fashion amongst patrons by the 1720s and any up-market retailer would have had to stock wares made in the French style in order to compete with rival goldsmiths. With a smart address behind the Royal Exchange, Folkingham would have been surrounded by some of the most fashionable goldsmith retailers and would have sold wares in the French style in order to compete with them.

[6] See E.A. Jones, *Catalogue of the Collection of Old Plate of William Francis Farrer* (London, 1924).
[7] Sothebys, Monaco, 1 December 1975, lot 256.
[8] Willaume's casket forms part of a toilet service of 26 items. It includes two paste pots which have exactly the same cast decorative panels as a pair in another toilet service, also of 1725, bearing the mark of Paul de Lamerie. J. Hayward, *Huguenot Silver in England, 1688–1727* (London, 1959), p. 42.

Although by the end of his lifetime it is obvious from the surviving objects that Folkingham was drawing on the skills and techniques introduced by foreign craftsmen, this does not appear to have been the case earlier on in his career. He signed two petitions complaining about the competition that had been created within the trade by 'necessitous strangers'. The first petition of 1711 complained that the alien goldsmiths were undercutting their English rivals, causing the English goldsmiths to work longer hours and charge less for their work. The second petition of about 1716 demonstrated against aliens who had not served an apprenticeship being allowed to have their wares assayed at Goldsmiths' Hall.

The signing of these petitions against the Huguenots suggests that from 1706 (the date when Folkingham first entered his mark) to at least 1716 (the date of the second petition), Folkingham would have been subcontracting his work only to English goldsmiths.[9] Hence, it is probable that between these dates the objects bearing Folkingham's mark are of English manufacture. The majority of these pieces are plain and rely on proportions rather than surface decoration for their effect (Fig. 36).[10]

A search of surviving items of plate which bore Folkingham's mark revealed a wide range of objects dating pre-1720 that would have been made or retailed at his first address. Twenty different types of object were found; these included candlesticks, casters, salvers and a number of items for hot drinks. This demonstrates that even at an early stage in his career Folkingham was acting as a retailer as well as running a workshop and therefore would have used subcontractors. No goldsmith could produce such a wide range of objects when so many different specialist skills and equipment would be needed for their manufacture.

Fig. 36. A teapot bearing the mark of Thomas Folkingham, 1711–12. The stand bearing the mark of Gabriel Sleath, 1712–13
(Tessiers Ltd.)

Other Orphans Court inventories in the sample confirm that Folkingham was indeed subcontracting work to English goldsmiths at this time. In 1714, Thomas Ash (known as a supplier of tea caddies and candlesticks) was owed £8. 18s. by 'Mr Fouringham'

---

[9] Anthony Nelme also signed the 1711 petition against the Huguenots but is known to have employed a Huguenot journeyman in 1706. Grimwade, *London Goldsmiths*, p. 760
[10] A.G. Grimwade, *The Queens Silver; a survey of Her Majesty's personal collection* (London: The Connoisseur, 1953), p. 25 describes Folkingham as 'a worthy representative of the native English goldsmiths who resisted the influences of their Huguenot rivals and continued to produce honest well-proportioned domestic silver for normal use'.

(Figs. 37 and 38).[11] A year later in 1715 'Mr ffalkingham' is recorded as being one of John Jackson's debtors, owing the later 14s. 6d.[12] Jackson, who ran both a workshop and acted as a retailer, may have been supplying Folkingham with wares from his workshop or with goods from his retailing business.

His inventory and extant objects imply that for the majority of his working career Folkingham was reliant on a network of English goldsmiths who acted as his suppliers and subcontractors, but also that Huguenot craftsmen played an increasingly important part in his career as his business grew and had therefore to meet the demands of a larger, more prosperous clientele.

Folkingham's inventory seems typical of the other twenty-four Orphans Court inventories studied, as surprisingly none of these inventories appear to include the names of any Huguenot goldsmiths, with one exception: in the inventory of Thomas Ash who died in 1714, Paul de Lamerie, the great Huguenot goldsmith, is listed amongst Ash's list of debtors (Fig. 37). Thus the inventories as a whole imply that the goldsmiths in the sample did not do business with Huguenot goldsmiths. But, as already shown with Folkingham, an analysis of the surviving objects bearing the sponsor's mark of goldsmiths in the sample, in terms of their decoration and form, reveals that a number of these objects show foreign influences. Thus the surviving objects contradict the impression of ethnic separation conveyed in the inventories.

It is strange that Huguenot craftsmen are not recorded in the inventories, especially given that the retail goldsmiths in the sample were dealing in goods in the foreign style and were dependent for much of their business on a network of subcontractors and suppliers working in different styles. There are several possible

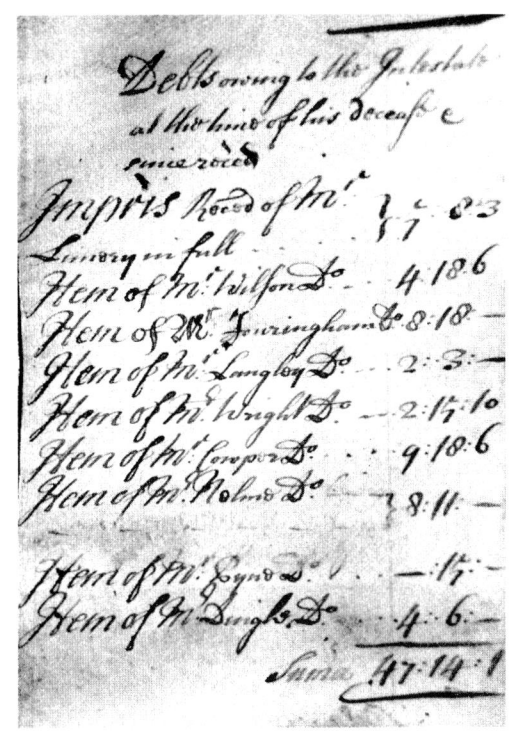

Fig. 37. Extract from the inventory of Thomas Ash, detailing his list of debtors.
(Corporation of London Records Office)

Fig. 38. A tea caddy bearing the mark of Thomas Ash.
(Tessiers Ltd.)

[11] CLRO, Orph. Inv. 2999 a and b, Thomas Ash.
[12] CLRO, Orph. Inv. 3005, John Jackson.

explanations as to why they are omitted from the inventories and yet their influence can be detected on surviving objects in terms of style or technique. It may be that foreign goldsmiths were employed as outworkers, but were paid immediately for work done rather than working on the same credit system as their English counterparts, although it is unlikely that all business would have been conducted on this basis. Another possible theory is that the English goldsmiths were employing foreigners in their workshops and paying them a journeyman's wage. Possibly some foreign craftsmen adopted English derivations of their names and therefore have not been identified in the inventories. An example of this can be seen with the Jewish goldsmith Abraham Oliveyra who came to England in 1685 — five different variations of his name are known.[13]

Alternatively English goldsmiths may have been working indirectly with the aliens, marking the wares of foreigners as their own in return for a small fee. This seems credible — certainly for the goldsmiths in the sample whose inventories date around the end of the seventeenth century — due to the fact that it was difficult at the end of the century for foreign craftsmen to obtain their freedom from the Goldsmiths' Company and mark their own wares. However, it seems unlikely that this was still the case by 1730. The inventories run from 1694 to 1732 and it is most likely that by the end of this period English goldsmiths would have mastered many of the Huguenot skills and techniques themselves or would have had access to foreign design sources. It may simply be a matter of 'geography' which explains the lack of the Huguenots appearing in the debtors and creditors lists. During this period, the majority of Huguenot goldsmiths were based in the Soho area while all the goldsmiths in the sample taken were freemen and worked in the City of London, with the majority of them being situated around Goldsmiths' Hall and Lombard Street. Further research may show that it is geographical location that explains the discrepancies between the inventories and the surviving objects.

To conclude, the inventories studied show the exclusion of aliens from their lists of debtors and creditors, with the weight of the evidence pointing to the fact that the English goldsmiths in the sample were not dealing with foreign craftsmen but formed part of a small, closely-knit community tied together by social and business relationships which relied on a closed network of English goldsmiths for the success of their businesses. This implies that the absolute division in the trade between English and alien goldsmiths still applied between the years of 1694 and 1732. Yet when an analysis was made of the surviving objects for Folkingham and other goldsmiths in the sample who possessed a sponsor's mark, a distinct foreign influence was seen, indicating that aliens did play an intrinsic part, either practically or stylistically, in the business lives of the English goldsmiths. In this respect, the objects highlight one of the limitations of relying on inventories as evidence. No definite conclusions can be drawn to reconcile the evidence of the inventories with the evidence of the surviving objects, but ultimately the goldsmith had no choice but to provide goods in the styles demanded by their customers by one means or another.

---

[13] Oliveyra is recorded in the Poor Rate Books in 1739/40 as 'Oliver'; Guildhall Library, London, MS 5419, vols. 41 and 42.

'The King's Arms and Feathers'. A case study exploring the networks of manufacture operating in the London goldsmiths' trade in the eighteenth century

Helen Clifford

The study of silver has been traditionally the province of the museum and the private collector. The main source has been the individual objects in collections which has resulted in a body of scholarship that concentrates on the object, the source of its design and the biography of the smith who made it. One consequence of this approach is that the activities of design and making have been explained in terms of the talents of individual designers and craftsmen. Two assumptions underpin much of the existing literature: first, the assumption that the objects which survive in museums and other collections are representative of the total output of any particular silversmithing business; and second, the assumption that production was undertaken directly by master craftsmen working (with assistants) in their workshops on commissions for high quality silverware.[1] These assumptions have generated a literature in which the design and manufacture of silverware is judged as Art rather than Commerce, the product of aesthetics rather than of profit. The purpose of this paper is to contest these assumptions by examining some of the work produced by one partnership of silversmiths in the second half of the eighteenth century and the ways in which that work was undertaken.

From the mid nineteenth century any discussion of the organisation of production in the goldsmiths' trade would have been written in terms of the background and training of master craftsmen, in the light of any silver that could be identified as theirs. It is an approach which is the result of a stress on the importance of the maker's marks, the identification and interpretation of which, first by Octavius Morgan in 1853, and secondly with the publication of William Chaffer's *Hallmarks on Gold and Silver Plate* in 1863 and his *Gilda Aurifabrorum* in 1883, were the foundation of scholarly studies in silver (Fig. 39). To be able to authenticate not only the date but the maker of an object is rare in the decorative arts.[2] The ability to do so promoted the study of silver into the province of the fine arts, which at that time was preoccupied with problems of authorship and authenticity. The spotlight is now on the interaction and

---

[1] The majority of silversmiths were men, but see P. Glanville and J.F. Goldsborough, *Women Silversmiths 1685–1845. Works from the Collection of The National Museum of Women in the Arts Washington, D.C.* (London, 1990).

[2] See J. Culme, 'Attitudes to Old Plate 1750–1900', in *The Directory of Gold and Silversmiths, 1834–1914* (2 vols., Woodbridge, 1987).

interdependence within the goldsmiths' trade, rather than on the biography of individuals. This paper is in itself a product of this shift in approach.

For the rest of this paper I am going to focus on one goldsmithing business, that of John Parker and Edward Wakelin, to see how they organised the manufacture and supply of silverware to their 291 account customers. The cumulative evidence contained in this publication should prove that their methods were neither unique to the goldsmiths' trade nor to the eighteenth century.

In 1735 George Wickes moved to Panton Street off the Haymarket and opened the 'King's Arms and Feathers'.[3] His goldsmithing business became one of the largest and most prosperous in London. It developed from its foundation through successive partnerships: from 1750 George Wickes and Samuel Netherton; from 1760 John Parker (Samuel Netherton's second cousin, apprenticed to Wickes in 1751)[4] and Edward Wakelin; from 1776 John Wakelin (Edward's son) and William Paris Tayler; and on Tayler's death in 1792 John Wakelin and Robert Garrard. The story of the firm is preserved in an unrivalled set of accounts dealing with clients and manufacturers, known collectively as the Garrard Ledgers.[5] The Ledgers represent the debt books, where 'all books mentioned before centre, and are as it were, copied or repeated'. As the last stage in the accounting procedure they are, as Defoe remarked, 'the register of [the tradesman's] estate, the index of his stock; all the tradesman has in the world must be found in these articles'.[6]

Fig. 39. The mark of John Parker and Edward Wakelin, 1770–1.
(W.R.T. Wilkinson & Robert Baker)

When the Gentlemen's or clients' accounts are matched with the Workmen's or suppliers' accounts, which can be done for the years 1766 to 1770, it can be seen that there is no evidence to suggest that the firm had any manufacturing or repair facilities. It subcontracted all commissions to outworkers or suppliers who also supplied items for stock.

The five-year period 1766 to 1770 covers the middle years of John Parker and Edward Wakelin's partnership. The words 'Make and Sell' and the range of goods and services on their 1761 trade card (Fig. 40) conform to a standard format used by many

---

[3] E. Barr, *George Wickes 1698–1761 Royal Goldsmith* (London, 1980).
[4] E. Barr, 'John Parker, Gentleman and Goldsmith', *Apollo* (February 1988), pp. 94–5.
[5] See A.G. Grimwade, 'The Garrard Ledgers', a paper read before the Society of Silver Collectors, 10 April 1961 published in *The Proceedings of the Society of Silver Collectors* (1961). The Ledgers were discovered in 1952; they are now deposited in the Archive of Art and Design (Victoria and Albert Museum). Microfilm of the Ledgers from 1735 to 1818 can be consulted in the National Art Library or in the Department of Metalwork.
[6] Daniel Defoe, *The Complete English Tradesman* (London, 1726).

Fig. 40. Trade card of John Parker and Edward Wakelin, 1761.
(Archives Department, Westminster City Libraries)

goldsmiths at the time.[7] It sheds little light on the realities of manufacture and supply. Their first partnership contract, dated 11 October 1760, agrees to their relationship as co-partners and joint dealers in the 'Art Trade Mystery or Business of a Goldsmith, that is to say, in buying, selling, uttering, vending and retailing of all sorts of Wrought Plate, all such other Things as are usually sold by men of that Trade and Imployment'.[8] Nowhere in the contract does the word 'make' or 'manufacture' appear. Wickes and Netherton were paid £200 'for and in consideration of their quitting the ... shop' and a further £200 for the purchase of fixtures within the shop which included shelves and showcases but no tools. The detailed description of the shop appended to the contract confirms the idea that the 'King's Arms and Feathers' at this date was a retailing outlet with no workshop.

In order to minimise the cost of permanently employing a specialised workforce, and to maximise the extent of the services offered by the business on a flexible basis, Parker and Wakelin operated not a workshop but a network of specialised subcontractors.

---

[7] See Banks and Heal Collection, British Museum. For example, the trade cards of the goldsmith and jeweller Basil Denn, the jewellers and toymen Henry Morris, Charles Store and Richard Severn, and the jeweller George Robertson.

[8] Shrewsbury Record Office 2868/93. Partnership agreement, 1760.

Of the seventy-five subcontractors who appear in the Workmen's Ledgers between 1766 and 1770 thirty-seven are silversmiths. Those who supplied particular types of silverware can be divided into makers of candlesticks (John Arnell and Ebenezer Coker, who made the 'step pillar' variety), cups and covers (David Whyte), épergnes and tureens (Thomas Pitts), panakins and papboats (Walter Brind), spurs (Benjamin Cowper), cruets and casters (John Daniell, Francis Chanel, Robert Piercy and Thomas Nash) and silver furniture for cases and canisters (John Westry and Edward Darvis). William Lestourgeon, and later his son Aaron supplied various types of small work like funnels, tea tubs and bottle stands (Fig. 41).

The manufacture of flatware has always required specialist tools. Flatware as a separate craft in itself was subdivided into haft, spoon, fork, and knife and blade makers. The eighteenth century witnessed the appearance of a whole new range of decorative options which in turn became further specialist subdivisions. There were five flatware specialists amongst Parker and Wakelin's suppliers. William Portal was the sole supplier of 'octagon threaded' hafts. Thomas Squire specialised in green ivory hafts and steel blades. Isaac Callard's account reveals that he usually supplied sets of forks and spoons at a standard cost for his labour, for example making twelve table forks of the four-pronged variety cost 21s. James Tookey supplied tea and salt spoons of the 'common' variety, usually destined for the sales shop which he supplied on a regular basis. He charged 4s. a dozen for these standard tea spoons. The Chawners in contrast supplied decorated spoons with fluted handles and shell bowls.

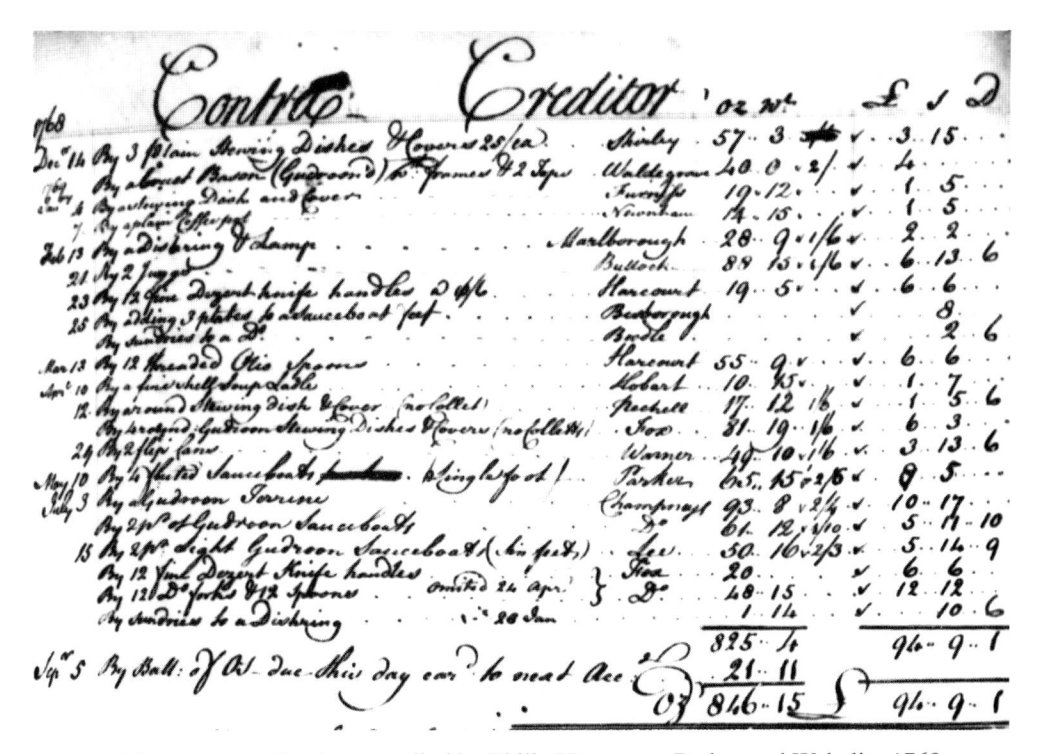

Fig. 41. Wrought plate supplied by Philip Norman to Parker and Wakelin, 1768.
(Victoria and Albert Museum)

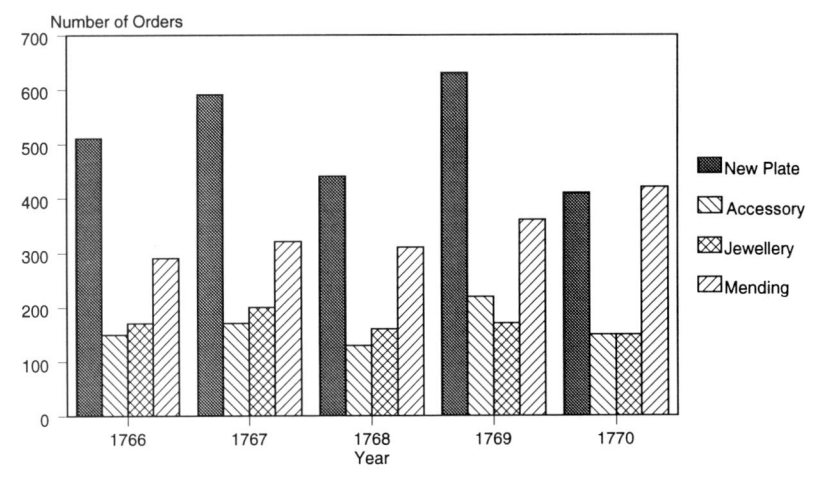

Fig. 42. Number of orders delivered to account customers divided by type, 1766 to 1770.

Source: Gentlemen's Ledger VAM7, Victoria and Albert Museum

Jewellery, apart from gold rings, was exempt from the Assay and therefore rarely bears the mark of the maker or supplier. As a result it is impossible to gain an impression, let alone calculate the size of Parker and Wakelin's jewellery trade from surviving objects.[9] The aggregate figures from the Ledgers reveal that it was a small but essential part of the business (Fig. 42). The sale of jewellery which was largely to commission and rarely for stock relied on nineteen jewellers and associated craftsmen. Of these, two were seal makers, two watchmakers and two bead stringers. Francis and John Creuze and John Wood supplied all Parker and Wakelin's precious stones and pearls. Isaac Rivière, John Barbot and Elias Russell specialised in gold work. The partnership of Louis Toussaint and James Morisset was responsible for all the orders involving enamelling. Six jewellers, Gideon Ernest Charpentier, Thomas Forrest, Michael Shucknell, Edward Holmes, Thomas Howell and Daniel Payan were paid for non-itemised work.

Plated wares came from John Derusat in Dean Street, from four Sheffield firms,[10] and Boulton and Fothergill in Birmingham. Other suppliers included Robert Clee, an engraver, two plate chest makers, a pocket book maker, three gilders and a knife case maker.

As well as craftsmen who specialised in particular techniques or objects there were those who provided the bulk of Parker and Wakelin's orders, supplying a wide range of large and small work in quantity. Aldridge and Woodnorth, Whipham and Wright, Smith and Sharp, Vincent and Lawford and to a greater extent Ansill and Gilbert were

---

[9] The Plate Offence Act of 1738 exempted a considerable number of minor articles weighing less than ten pennyweights from the assay including thimbles, toothpick cases and nutmeg graters, as well as any gold and silverware that might be damaged by marking because of its smallness or thinness or because it was 'so richly engraved, carved or chased, or set with Jewels or other Stones' that it was in danger of being damaged during the process of marking.

[10] Tudor and Leader, Robert, Elam and Winter, and later John Winter alone, Hancock and Sons, and Hoyland.

the partnerships on whom the business largely rested. The role of Ansill and Gilbert is of such importance that it will be dealt with in detail later.

A third category of suppliers can be identified, those who provided raw materials. The partnership of Spindler and Palmer was Parker and Wakelin's main source of refined silver until they began using Robert Albion Cox in 1769.

Given the number and importance of these subcontractors it is worth investigating their location in relation to the 'King's Arms and Feathers'.[11] Twenty of the subcontractors were located within a quarter of a mile radius from the 'King's Arms and Feathers', including Ansill and Gilbert and Robert Clee in Panton Street itself; William Portal in Orange Street; Elias Russell and Philip Rainaud in Suffolk Street; Philip Norman, Langford and Sebille and Hammond and Company in St. Martin's Lane. Sixteen subcontractors came from the environs of the Assay Office, including the Hennells, Robert Piercy, Walter Brind and Edward Holmes in Foster Lane; Margaret Binley and Spindler and Palmer in Gutter Lane; and Thomas Nash and John Wood in Noble Street. Nine operated from other areas within the Cities of London and Westminster and the Borough of Southwark. Butty and Dumee, Ebenezer Coker and David Whyte were based in Clerkenwell Close, the Chawners in Red Lion Street, Emick Romer in High Holborn, Isaac Rivière in Tottenham Court Road and Francis and John Creuze in Broad Street. William Cripps was the only supplier based in St. James's, in King Street. The Sheffield suppliers and Bolton and Fothergill form a fourth group, working outside London. Due to lack of surviving documentation twenty-three of the subcontractors remain without a known address.

Between 1766 and 1773 Parker and Wakelin subcontracted work to between thirty-four and sixty suppliers each year. When a number of large orders came in, as in 1768 with eleven clients requesting dinner services, Parker and Wakelin could involve the relevant craftsmen.

The silverware sold by Parker and Wakelin was marked either by them or by the supplier if he had registered a mark at Goldsmiths' Hall, or sometimes by both when overstamping occurs. The extent to which some goldsmiths sold wares made by others can be demonstrated by tracing the makers of the constituent parts of a dinner service supplied by one goldsmith's business. Part of the Harcourt Collection of silver which was sold at Sotheby's in June 1994 provides an excellent example of the manipulation of a complex network of suppliers by Parker and Wakelin.[12] Following Simon 1st Earl Harcourt's appointment as Ambassador to Paris in 1768 he ordered a service of plate from Parker and Wakelin. His account for 13 March that year which dealt with the order amounted to £3,862. 11s. 2d. In the Sotheby's sale some of the silver is unmarked, some bears the mark of Parker and Wakelin, and some pieces the marks of various subcontractors, like the silver gilt dessert service comprising twelve spoons and forks with the mark of Thomas and William Chawner, and twelve knives, the hafts of which are marked by Philip Norman. The twelve ladles or 'Olio Spoons' supplied by Norman

---

[11] Source of addresses: A. Grimwade, *London Goldsmiths 1697–1837* (3rd edn.; London, 1989); Sun Insurance Registers; Trade Directories 1765–1776; and *Report of the Committee Appointed to Enquire into the Manner of Conducting the Several Assay Offices*, 1773.

[12] See also sale of items from Stanton Harcourt in *Silver at Partridge*, October 1993.

Fig. 43. Dessert knife, fork and spoon from a thirty-six piece set, bearing the mark of Thomas and William Chawner, the knife handles by Philip Norman. Part of the Harcourt service, 1769.
(Partridge)

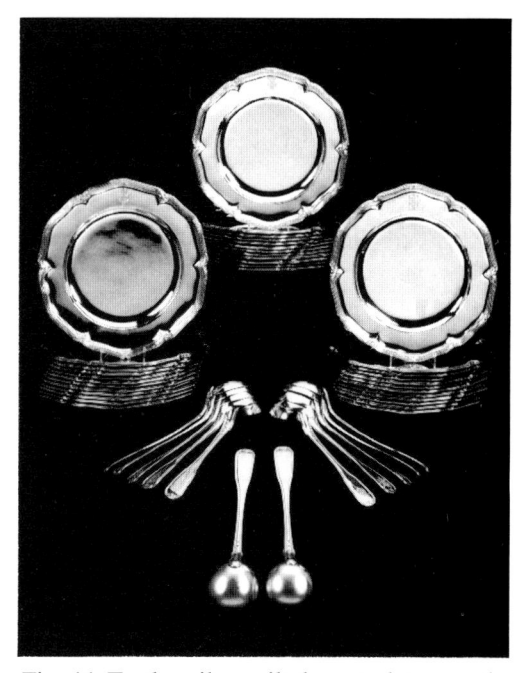

Fig. 44. Twelve silver-gilt dessert plates, mark of Parker and Wakelin, London 1768 and twelve silver-gilt ladles, mark of Philip Norman, London 1768. Supplied as part of the Harcourt service.
(Sotheby's)

for the same order cost Parker and Wakelin £6. 6s. They charged Lord Harcourt £15. 18s. 6d. in addition to an extra £17. 8s. for making and gilding them (Figs. 43 and 44).[13] The Ledgers reveal that David Hennell and Sons supplied the salts, Ansill and Gilbert made the plates, dishes and candlesticks, and Thomas Pitts supplied the épergnes.

A similar pattern of contracting out work to specialists can be seen in the supply of a toilet service to the Empress Elizabeth of Russia in 1757 by Samuel Courtauld. Only seven of the thirty-five pieces listed in the 1908 catalogue bear Courtauld's mark. Elias Cachet, Daniel Piers and Pierre Gillois were responsible for the other articles.[14] What does not survive is the information to show how the transmission of designs between subcontractors worked.

The subcontractors fall into two major categories, dependents like Ansill and Gilbert who seem to have relied on one firm for most, if not all their trade, and independent suppliers who either had their own retail outlets and/or supplied other businesses. However, it is impossible to know the exact balance between independent and dependent work. Defoe in his *Complete English Tradesman* provides a useful guide to these categories: 'those who make the goods they sell, though they keep shops' (whom he classified as handicraftsmen), 'those who only make goods for others to sell' (whom he

---

[13] *The Harcourt Collection* (Sotheby's, London, Thursday 10 June 1993), p. 9.
[14] E.A. Jones, *Silver Wrought by the Courtauld Family* (Oxford, 1940), p. 26.

calls manufacturers and artists), and those 'who do not actually manufacture the goods they sell' (tradesmen). Although Chaffers believed that the marks in the registers at Goldsmiths' Hall related to 'the names of actual manufacturers', which now needs to be reviewed, he attempted a clear explanation of the broad divisions within the craft: 'there are necessarily in every piece of decorative plate three parties to whom credit of production must be ascribed, viz. the artist who designs it, the plateworker who makes it, and the goldsmith who sells it and becomes the publisher'.[15]

The subcontracting network operated not only at the level of composite large scale orders but also on the smaller scale of individual objects. The supply of a particular type of tea caddy, referred to in the Ledgers as a 'tea tub' demonstrates how the system operated (Fig. 45). Aldridge and Woodnorth or, more usually, Ansill and Gilbert made the body of the tea tub using small working techniques of scoring, folding and soldering. The advent of the flatting mill made the supply of flat rolled sheet to an even gauge cheap and easy (compared to hand hammering from the ingot). The cube form itself was quick and cheap to make compared with the more time-consuming raising method required for earlier designs of tea canister. Ansill and Gilbert also supplied the cast finials, in a choice of three sizes of 'sprig': small, medium and large, which were attached to the lid by means of a silver nut. The tubs were then passed to Aaron and William Lestourgeon for locks to be fitted and the interior lined with lead.[16] After lining the chinese figures and border were engraved probably by Robert Clee, who lived opposite the 'King's Arms and Feathers'.[17] The last part of the order concerned the case if one was required, from Edward Smith.

Fig. 45. Tea tub bearing the mark of William and Aaron Lestourgeon, 1770.
(Ashmolean Museum)

So the '2 square tea tubs', supplied to Richard Cox weighing 26 oz 7 dwt (costing £7. 7s. 2d. in silver), had thus been made by Ansill and Gilbert (£4. 4s.), been sent to the Lestourgeons for locks and linings to be fitted (£6. 6s.), then delivered to the engraver for the 'graving of Characters' which was included in the cost for the locks and lining, and '2 Coats' (10s.) and had been delivered in a 'Plain Mahogany Case' costing 12s. The total order cost Richard Cox £18. 9s. 2d. It seems likely, from the prevalence of William and Aaron Lestorgeon's mark on surviving tea tubs that they were responsible

---

[15] W. Chaffers, *Gilda Aurifabrorum* (1883), pp. 167–8.
[16] Aaron Lestourgeon began to work alone sometime in 1769, and in the Sun Insurance Records appears at Toussaint and Morisset's in 1777. The latter partnership supplied the Panton Street business with enamelled and gold work.
[17] Robert Barker 'Robert Clee', a paper read before the Society of Silver Collectors, 1990.

for overseeing their passage through the various processes of manufacture and decoration.

Surviving tea tubs of this particular design between 1761 and 1770 can all, so far, be associated with Parker and Wakelin. It is unclear how Parker and Wakelin managed to control the use of the design which was both fashionable and profitable to make. The design itself originates from the chests in which the tea was imported, and appears in grocers' trade cards.

The complex network of seventy-five subcontractors that Parker and Wakelin used suggests that the practice was not an innovation of the partnership. Evidence survives in the form of a ledger, to confirm the idea that Wakelin was associated with Wickes, not in the position of a waged journeyman or a partner, but as a subcontractor himself, based in a workshop rented, and later bought for £400, from Wickes.[18] The ledger, catalogued as for stock, and called by Elaine Barr the Associates Ledger, has in her words been 'something of a conundrum'. It seems clear on detailed examination to be a record of the goods and services Wakelin supplied to Wickes, and later to Wickes and Netherton. The large amounts of money and weight of silver involved suggest a high level of interdependency. In 1749, 4,717 ounces of silver were owed to Wickes by Wakelin, and £647 owed to Wakelin by Wickes. In 1755, 15,328 ounces of silver were owed to Wickes and Netherton by Wakelin, and £1,182 owed to Wakelin by the partners.

Edward Wakelin, the son of a baker from Uttoxeter had been apprenticed to the Huguenot goldsmith John Hugh Lesage in 1730.[19] It is likely that Wakelin had begun supplying Wickes's business from 1744, when Wickes had bought a second building, next door but one to the 'King's Arms and Feathers' in Panton Street. It would have been a suitable time for Wickes to cease manufacture from the 'King's Arms and Feathers', keeping it solely as a sales shop and home. 1744 was a critical year for Wickes. By that date all his apprentices and turnovers (except John Parker, who had joined him in 1751) had completed their training with him. It would have been an ideal moment for Wakelin to take over the responsibility for the supply of goods.

Wakelin was not acting as a partner in the business. It was Samuel Netherton, who had been apprenticed to Wickes in 1737/8 who became a partner in the firm in 1750. Wakelin had entered his own mark at Goldsmiths' Hall in 1747 (giving his address as Panton Street), and not a joint one with Wickes, although both their marks are deceptively similar, consisting of gothic initials surmounted by three feathers. Furthermore in September 1748, Wakelin claimed his freedom of the Goldsmiths' Company in order to take his first apprentice, James Ansill.[20] Wakelin continued taking apprentices in his own right while supplying Wickes (Nathanial Bray, son of a

---

[18] Victoria and Albert Museum, Stock Ledger VAM4 (1747–60), Wakelin's supply ledger, comparable to that of the Crespell's supply ledger in layout.

[19] Corporation of London Records Office (CLRO), Indenture signed 3 June 1730 'Edward Wakelin Son of Edward Wakelin late of Uttoxeter in the County of Stafford Baker doth put himself Apprentice to John Lesage', premium £20.

[20] Goldsmiths' Company, Apprentice Book 1740–63, no.7, p. 106: 7 September 1748, son of James Ansill of the parish of Stow in the County of Stafford Husbandman. Free 1 January 1764.

diamond cutter in Lothbury in 1750,[21] Stephen Gilbert in 1752,[22] John Arnell was turned over to him in 1758 having begun his apprenticeship with John Quantock a candlestick maker six years before).[23]

Between 1749 and 1759 Wakelin controlled a sizeable workforce, all of whom appear to be training or working goldsmiths. The Ledger records that Wakelin employed at least seven men, who were paid a regular wage over relatively short periods of time, from four months to two and a half years. The wages of Abraham Potts, William Collipress, John Griffen and David Edwards were usually paid on a yearly basis at about £5. 10s. to £8 per annum. The amounts suggest they performed unskilled work and were not journeymen. James Ansill and Stephen Gilbert seem to have been employed in this capacity before beginning their apprenticeships with Wakelin at the relatively late age of seventeen.[24] It is interesting to note that the regional bias in favour of Staffordshire as a source of apprentices, begun by Wakelin is continued by Ansill and Gilbert, who took on Randolph Jones of Church Stretton and Charles Hulme from Uttoxeter.

In the same ledger are the names of twelve men paid by Wakelin between 1747 and 1760, who by their pay and the type of work they executed must have been skilled. They were paid according to bills of work they submitted, and concerned different manufacturing processes rather than the supply of finished or part-finished products (apart from Andrew Killick who provided candlesticks). John Fisher submitted bills for chasing work every six to eight months from 1756. Wakelin paid him in a combination of ready money, silver taken off articles and pit tickets.[25] William Soloman who had registered his mark at Goldsmiths' Hall as a plateworker in October 1747 worked for Wakelin from at least February that year. Soloman specialised in cast work, flatting and piercing. George Elger a turner was frequently paid in waste from the 'melt of short turnings'. Entries for Elger begin in February 1747, and continue until September 1759. From Samuel Paddison's accounts which begin in March 1754 it seems that he was a skilled polisher. His bills were paid regularly in March, June, September and December each year. Cornelius Woldring submitted regular bills for casting and burnishing from 1749, and his account, like many of the others was closed a few days before Parker and Wakelin's partnership contract was signed.

The combination of apprentices, waged employees and outside suppliers ensured that Wakelin had access to a flexible workforce of between eight to thirteen men at any one time between 1747 and 1760. On the day that Parker and Wakelin's partnership took effect, 11 October 1760, the lease of the workshop, along with patterns and fixtures worth £400 (the same amount that Wakelin had paid Wickes twelve years previously)

---

[21] Ibid., p. 136. 2 May 1750, son of Nathaniel Bray late of Parish of St Mary Lothbury London Diamond Cutter. 20 September 1753 turned over to William Priest Goldsmith. Premium £30. Free 7 February 1759.
[22] Ibid., p. 176. 8 May 1752, son of John Gilbert late of Hixton in the County of Stafford yeoman. Free 1 February 1764.
[23] Ibid., p. 183. 5 October 1752, son of John Arnell of Paddington in the County of Middlesex, weaver apprentice to John Quantock. Turned over to Edward Wakelin on 6 December 1758.
[24] Guildhall Library, International Geneaological Index, 'James Ancil, son of James Ancil, christened 4th July 1731 at Stowe'. 'Stephen Gilbert, son of John Gilbert, christened 23rd January 1734 at Stowe'.
[25] Silver 'season tickets' to the theatre.

was transferred to John Christopher Romer, a silver chaser who had been supplying Wakelin since at least 1752.[26]

In 1760 all Wakelin's apprentices and turnovers had completed their training. Perhaps this implies a long-term planning strategy in operation? In his new capacity as partner Wakelin took only two further apprentices, Thomas Boswood, the son of an undertaker in 1762 and in March 1766 John Kinnaird who had begun his apprenticeship with Simon Gordon, an upholder in June 1762. His last apprentice was his son John, his indenture is dated 5 March 1766.[27] John Parker took only one apprentice, Daniel Flowerdew in 1762.[28] It is probable that these apprentices worked in the sales shop, and were not involved in manufacture.

On 1 February 1764 it seems likely that James Ansill and Stephen Gilbert assumed responsibility for the workshop that Wakelin had once controlled. On this day they were both made free of the Goldsmiths' Company, and began taking their own apprentices and turnovers, at a rate of almost one a year between 1764 and 1772. Unfortunately, the first Workmen's Ledger of Parker and Wakelin's partnership does not survive, so the exact arrangements and dates are unknown. The earliest reference to Ansill and Gilbert's rent of the workshop from Parker and Wakelin is 17 October 1767 when 'a Years Rent & taxes to Michaelmas £40. 0s. 10d.' is recorded. Between 1768 and 1769 they supplied 318 orders of over 25,000 troy ounces in weight costing Parker and Wakelin over £2,000 for their labour. These figures should be set against the total weight of wrought silver supplied by Parker and Wakelin during the same period which was 33,579 troy ounces.[29] Ansill and Gilbert in their turn were replaced by James and Sebastian Crespell as the major suppliers to the Panton Street business in 1772. The Panton Street workshop remained the major source of silverware and services for the business until 1779 when it was transferred to the corner of Oxendon Street. Wakelin retained possession of the Panton Street workshop until his retirement in 1776.

To summarise, in the history of the firm there were two separate concepts, first plateworking which involved the manufacture and supply of silverware, and secondly retailing involving sales and admininstration. The two activities were often divided between individuals or partnerships. Wickes and Netherton relinquished the responsibility of manufacture and supply to Wakelin in the 1740s, while they concentrated on the increasingly specialised task of administration. The pattern was repeated in the 1760s and 1770s when Ansill and Gilbert took over Wakelin's workshop while Parker and Wakelin controlled sales and credit control.

---

[26] Emick Romer, who was probably an older brother, or cousin of John Christopher supplied the firm with sugar baskets from 1770. Grimwade, *London Goldsmiths*, p.766.

[27] Goldsmiths' Company, Apprentice Book No.8, p. 80, '5th March 1766 John Wakelin son of Edward Wakelin of Panton Street in the County of Middlesex, Goldsmith'.

[28] Goldsmiths' Company, Apprentice Book No.7 1740-63, p. 329 (on the same page as John Kinnaird), 9th June 1762, son of Nathaniel Flowerdew now residing in parts beyond the seas. Premium £50.

[29] Parker and Wakelin's output for 1768/9 can be compared with the London Assay Office totals for the same period. The total amount assayed was 95,909 troy pounds, 1,046 troy pounds were broken. Source: *Report of the Committee Appointed to Enquire into the manner of Conducting the Several Assay Offices*, 1773.

It is certain that Wickes was familiar with the use of a subcontractor network even before the 1740s. A detailed inventory of 1729 relating to the business of Thomas Folkingham lists the value of shop goods at £1,650, ready money and household goods at £2,092, but makes no reference to a workshop.[30] It is apparent that Folkingham had been running a retail establishment which relied on suppliers who are listed as creditors to the business. Both George Wickes, and his first partner before his arrival at Panton Street, John Craig were witnesses to the inventory. Furthermore, George Pitches a close kinsman of Wickes had been apprenticed to Folkingham in 1706.

Out of the attempt to discover what the so-called 'maker's mark' represented has come a picture of a changing relationship between maker, retailer and object. During the eighteenth century it seems that the London goldsmiths' trade was composed of three groups: first, those who manufactured goods such as plateworkers, smallworkers and goldworkers; second, manufacturers who also retailed; and third, businesses that retailed only and had no facility for making any of their own wares. They were tied together by their mutual dependence on each other's skills. The acquisition of materials, the contracting-out of work, the sale of goods, the negotiation of credit, the hiring of journeymen and the creation and preservation of co-operation between masters and men meant that workshop organisation extended beyond the production of vendible commodities. In the context of a trade characterised by the exchange of skill, of information, of raw materials and castings, where a finished object may have passed through several hands, the idea that single pieces have individual authorship needs to treated with considerable scepticism.

---

[30] CLRO, Orphans Inventory 3330. I am grateful to Robert Barker for drawing my attention to this document.

The design of London goldsmiths' shops in the early eighteenth century

CLAIRE WALSH

This paper examines the appearance of goldsmiths' shops in London during the first half of the eighteenth century. It aims to show how goldsmiths displayed goods in their shops, how they designed their interiors, and what part design and display played in attracting customers and in marketing both the shop and the goods it sold. The focus is on four areas: display fittings, interior design, the business identity of shops, and shops geared to down-market selling. [1]

Interior Fittings and Display

Unfortunately very few images survive that provide information about the appearance of eighteenth-century goldsmiths' shop interiors. Nevertheless, there is a trade card from the 1750s for the goldsmith Phillips Garden (Fig. 46). This shows an impressive interior, with a large shop window on the left, a gothic screen on the right, and at the back of the shop behind a long counter, a glass display cabinet which stretches the full length of the wall. To what extent, however, does this image present a realistic representation of an eighteenth-century goldsmith's shop? To what extent did goldsmiths use display and interior design in their shops, and how important a tool were display and design for the retailing goldsmith?

Other sources which can help establish the appearance of eighteenth-century goldsmith shops are inventories, plans, court records and contemporary comment. Inventories from the Orphans Court, surviving from the late seventeenth century to the 1730s, and from the Public Record Office, from the 1740s onwards, list standard items found in all goldsmiths' shops: counters, measuring instruments such as scales, and chairs for customers.[2] These items might be termed basic shopkeeping equipment and they appear in inventories for other types of shops as well. This essential shopkeeping equipment distinguishes retail shops from workshops where such items are not listed, and they make it clear that the retail shop is a specialised environment geared to the specific activity of selling.

As well as the practical items of shopkeeping, a range of display fittings used by goldsmiths also appear in the inventories such as show glasses, stall carpets, show

---

[1] This paper arises from part of my M.A. dissertation, 'Shop design and the display of goods in the eighteenth century', Royal College of Art, 1993.
[2] My survey of inventories covered twenty-one inventories for a variety of trades from 1695–1732, working trades list C, from the Orphans Court (Orph. Inv.) at the Corporation of London Records Office (CLRO) and sixteen inventories for various trades from 1742–1790 from Probate 31 at the Public Record Office (PRO), Chancery Lane.

Fig. 46. Trade card for Phillips Garden, goldsmith, 1750s.
(British Museum, Heal Collection)

boards, nests of drawers and presses. 'Show glasses' were significant items appearing in many of the retailing goldsmith inventories. These were glass display cases which came in a variety of sizes. Some were small enough to be placed in windows and on counters, and in one case on a table surrounded by nine chairs.[3] They are referred to frequently in court cases when stolen from open shop windows or from outside the shop where they had been placed to attract passing customers. A crime pamphlet from 1729 records the theft of a show glass from outside a shop which contained 'nine Silver Watches and one of Gold'.[4] A satirical print from the 1740s depicts what is

---

[3] CLRO, Orph. Inv. 2433, John Johnson.
[4] Anon, *The Life of Tho. Neaves, The Noted Street Robber* (1729), Guildhall Library, MS 14203.

Fig. 47. Detail of satirical print of 'A Lady's Disaster', 1740s.
(British Museum)

probably a small glass showcase placed on the street by a small-scale retailer to attract attention to his shop (Fig. 47). This particular case has six glass panes, but a goldsmith's inventory from 1728 records '4 Show Glasses for ye Windows containing 8 glasses Square'. Four cases of this size must have completely packed the retailer's window and made quite an impression. This shop also possessed '2 Hangings Glasses with 8 Squares' perhaps to be hung on the walls of the shop or behind the window.[5] Other show glasses appear to have been larger upright affairs, apparently like small cabinets; in court cases these are referred to as having glass tops and drawers beneath which held small items such as buttons and buckles.[6]

The importance of show glasses to retailing goldsmiths is evident not only from the regularity with which they appear in inventories, but also from the quantities with which they can occur in a single shop. Six show glasses are listed in an inventory from 1679, and seven in an inventory from 1742.[7] Sometimes velvet is recorded lining the drawers of the show glasses, and this emphasises the significance goldsmiths placed on the manner in which their goods were displayed and the consideration they gave to enhancing the appearance and presentation of their goods.

---

[5] CLRO, Orph. Inv. 3330, Andrew Dalton.

[6] For example, *The Old Bailey Proceedings*, February 1780 (Brighton, 1984), p. 180.

[7] CLRO, Orph. Inv. 1526, Philip Trahern, and PRO, PROB 31 230/714, John Body, respectively.

'Stall carpetts' and 'stall clothes' are terms which appear in inventories and possibly refer to the carpet or cloth used to line the display area in the shop window, to provide a rich and colourful background to the goods on show and to catch the eye of passers-by on the street.[8]

As well as using conventional showcases, retailers also responded imaginatively to the need to display: George Clarke, watchmaker, possessed in 1756 'a Glass Case with a large looking Glass plate and 56 brass hooks, 2 lead pulleys, a mahogany (sliding) door'. The fifty-six hooks were presumably for his watches, with the looking glass reflecting the workmanship on their reverse — the display fittings here were geared to show off the particular qualities of these goods to their best advantage.[9] A further alternative for displaying smaller and less expensive items in goldsmiths' shops were 'show boards', propped up on stands onto which goods could be hooked or pinned.[10] This method was far more commonly employed by other trades such as lacemen and milliners, and for goldsmiths the use of the more impressive and formal glass show cases was the more usual form of displaying goods.

Formality of presentation was a key function of the 'Nests of drawers' listed in many of the goldsmiths' inventories.[11] These were for keeping small items such as jewellery, watches or small toys. Individual drawers could be taken out and placed on the counter in front of the customer where they would act as a suitably dignified container for small, but possibly very expensive goods. In this way the value or special qualities of the goods were not undermined as might be the case with awkward manual handling or poor wrapping.

The most important method of display for the goldsmith, however, was the goldsmith's press. With only the odd exception, all goldsmiths' shops contained presses. These were large cupboards with open shelves and glass doors across the front. They are most often referred to in inventories as 'glass press' or press with 'sashes' and are distinct from simple shelving. It is the size and positioning of these presses which establishes their importance. Most often presses covered the whole of one wall of the shop, usually behind the counter, where they formed the key focus for customers in the shop. As most retailing goldsmiths' stock consisted predominantly of plate, most room in the shop was given over to keeping and prominently displaying this plate. Presses do not appear in the inventories of retailers who were primarily jewellers.

Although most goldsmiths' inventories are perfunctory in their detail, measurements of shop fittings are provided in two inventories for Martha Braithwaite's shop, both taken in 1746, which record two glass presses covering the whole of two facing sides of the shop.[12] Each press was 15 feet long and over 4 feet high and they contained between them over 113 square feet of glass and cost £8. 9s. 9d. Andrew Dalton's shop contained in 1728 '2 Goldsmiths presses fixed containing 80 Squares of Glass', which

---

[8] For example CLRO, Orph. Inv. 2233, Robert Hill, and CLRO, Orph. Inv. 2856, Michael Wilson.
[9] PRO, PROB 31 390/283, George Clarke.
[10] For example, see George Braithwaite, PRO, Chancery Masters Exhibits C105/5 Part I.
[11] 'Nests of drawers' occur in six of the goldsmiths' inventories from the CLRO, for example, see CLRO, Orph. Inv. 2587, Francis Greville.
[12] George Braithwaite, PRO, Chancery Masters Exhibit C105/5 Part I. I would like to thank David Mitchell for drawing my attention to this deposit.

suggests presses on the same scale as Braithwaite's.[13] This begins to throw more light on other goldsmiths' inventories, such as that for John Johnson from 1699, which merely lists 'Counter chests & presses ... 2 show glasses and covers', but values them at £25. 5s. 6d.[14] The high valuation can only point to the large extent of glazing in the presses, and this is frequently echoed in other inventories.

Goldsmiths' glass presses were central to a retailing goldsmith's trade. They allowed a large number of goods to be put on show to the customer, they framed the goods attractively and sought to enhance their appearance. Such lavishly expensive containers reflected and underlined the quality and value of the goldsmith's wares. While glass did provided a certain amount of security for the goldsmith, its prime quality was the impression it created. A very large amount of capital was tied up in a retailing goldsmith's stock, and the sheer expanse of the glass employed in glass presses, its expense and its prominence in the shop served not only to draw attention to this stock, but was also a vital expression of the financial standing of the goldsmith and thus reinforced the credibility of the stock on show and the credibility of the retailer.

Simply from the range of different display fittings and the expense and care expended on them, it is obvious that display was considered an important tool by the eighteenth-century goldsmith. Display fittings deployed in shop windows and on the street aimed to attract customers to the shop, and then, once they were inside, such fittings aimed to maintain their interest and conviction in the goods on sale.

Interior design

The details provided in Martha Braithwaite's inventories of 1746 are very useful in a further way. The measurements they provide allow a reasonable reconstruction of the layout of her shop and give us a good idea of the interior decoration of a goldsmith's shop in the first half of the eighteenth century (Fig. 48). The length of the cornice sets out the size of the shop; it ran all around the fore shop, 15 feet by 7 feet, which matches well with the layout of shops seen on plans for the same period. There were the two presses covering the whole of the east and the west sides of the shop, the area of glass used was approximately 4½ feet by 15 feet in each case, with the 'nest of drawers' and two shelves underneath the 'West Press'. The counter was 15 feet long, enclosing the retailer completely on her side of the shop. At the back end of the shop there were '2 Wooden Carvd Pillars with an Arch and 2 half arches', and there were 'Mouldings' at the front end of the shop. The cornice, which ran all around the shop, was 2 feet deep and was part painted and part gilded. There was a glass door between the fore shop and the back shop containing 15 square feet of glass, and there was a sash frame next to the stairs with 6 feet 10 inches square of glass. In addition, the shop was equipped with show boards on oak stands and 'Three Shew Glasses with Mahogony frames' with 3 square feet of glass in each which contained oak drawers 'lind with velvet'. The shop also possessed a dresser, a desk, and a cupboard with wainscot drawers.

---

[13] CLRO, Orph. Inv. 3330, Andrew Dalton.
[14] CLRO, Orph. Inv. 2433, John Johnson.

DESIGN OF LONDON GOLDSMITHS' SHOPS

S

7 ft

BACK SHOP

GLASS DOOR TO THE BACK SHOP
3x5 ft OF GLASS (10 PANES)

WINDOW BY THE STAIRS
2x3 ft

STAIRS

TWO WOODEN CARVED PILLARS
WITH AN ARCH+2 HALF ARCHES

E
15 ft

COUNTER - 15ft

W
15 ft

PRESS FOR PLATE
15x4 ft GLASS

PRESS FOR PLATE
15x4 ft OF GLASS DRAWERS+ SHELVES BENEATH

OTHER ITEMS

• *3 SHOW GLASSES 3 SQUARE FOOT OF GLASS IN EACH WITH DRAWERS LINED WITH VELVET*

• *SHEW BOARDS + OAK STANDS + HOLD FASTS*

• *A DRESSER, A DESK + CUPBOARD*

CORNICE
AROUND THE SHOP 2 ft DEEP PAINTED & GILT

MOULDINGS
ALONG FRONT OF SHOP

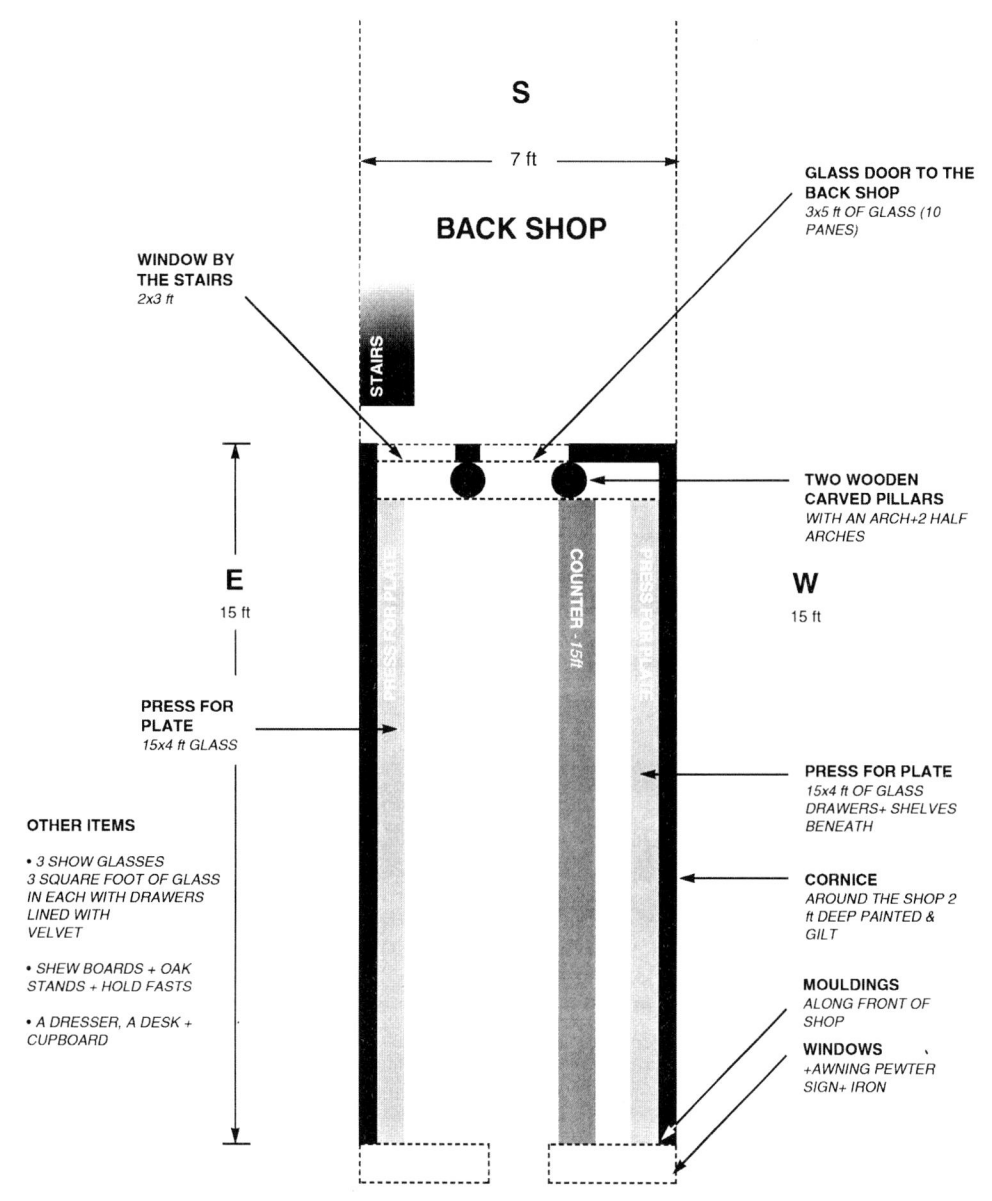

WINDOWS
+AWNING PEWTER SIGN+ IRON

Fig. 48. Reconstruction of Martha Braithwaite's goldsmith's shop based on Chancery Masters inventories from 1746 in the Public Record Office.

This description throws up some important features. Firstly, a significantly large proportion of the shop interior was given over to the display of goods — a full three sides of the shop, without including the show glasses. Secondly, the use of glass is impressive both in its quantity and with the front windows, in its impact on all four sides of the shop. Thirdly, there is the extensive use of interior decorative features; prominent pillars, arches, mouldings and gilded cornice. This kind of prominent interior decoration also appears in inventories for other kinds of shops, often with the arches dividing one section of the shop from another. A surviving screen dividing the fore and

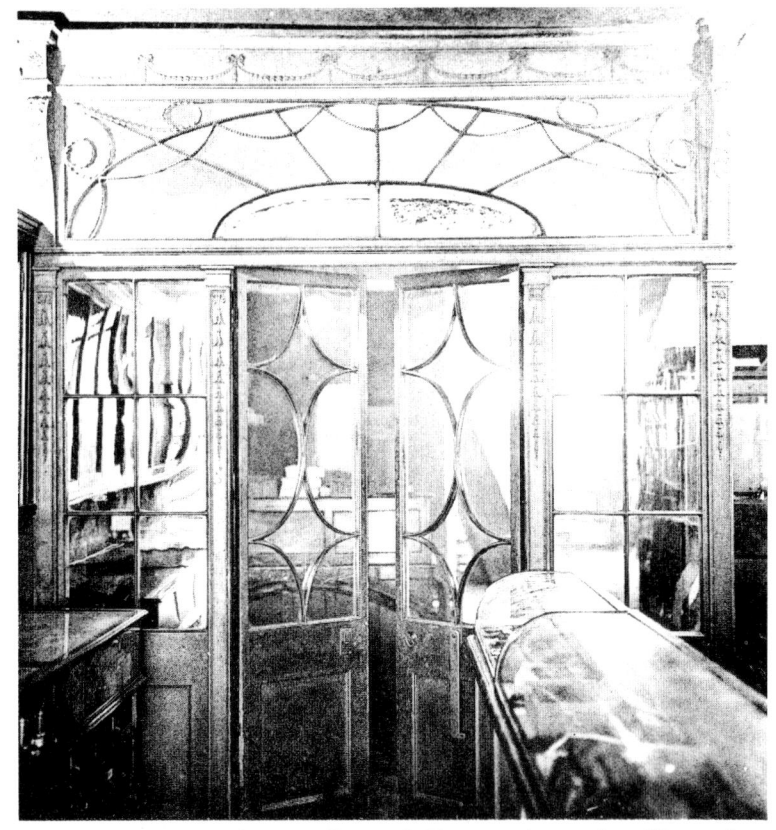

Fig. 49. Shop screen from Freibourg & Treyer, tobacconists, Haymarket, London, 1780s (now Paperchase).
(British Museum)

back shop of a tobacconist from the 1780s (Fig. 49), and in the height of fashion in the Neoclassical style, gives some idea of the visual impact the pillars, arches and glass door would have made in Braithwaite's shop.

Arches or screens would have been utilised to break up interior space, but more importantly, they made a grand design statement, reflecting or echoing the architectural gestures of up-market private homes and public interiors such as in assembly halls and at pleasure gardens. Such decorative elements created shop interiors which could be stylistically fashionable, socially specific, and visually dramatic. These sophisticated interiors were designed to attract the right level of customer and to retain their custom, which they could do only if they could keep up with fashion and with competition from other shops. These grand gestures of interior design must have changed frequently, as the fronts of shops did, with the latest fashion trends. Images created of classy, artistic interiors were superficial and contemporary commentators remarked on the theatricality of the capital's shops. In 1709 the drapers' shops on Ludgate Hill were described as 'perfect gilded theatres'.[15]

---

[15] Quoted in J.P. Malcolm, *Anecdotes of the manners and customs of London during the eighteenth century* (London, 1808), p. 133.

Returning to the representation of a goldsmith's shop in Phillips Garden's trade card (Fig. 46), it now seems that, although probably idealised for advertising purposes, this image is not, however, unrealistic. The press behind the counter probably represents a conventional display for plate for a high class London goldsmith, and beneath it are the nests of drawers for jewellery and small items. There is a substantial display of goods in the window. The elaborate carved screen, in up-to-date Gothic style, divides one part of the shop from another. If this is meant to have glass panes, then we can see glazing represented on three sides of the shop. Impressive though this image is, it still does not reveal the further range of display fittings which were available to goldsmiths in the eighteenth century; show glasses, stall clothes, and show boards. But this image does highlight the specialist nature of shop interiors and how effectively interiors could be geared to a particular market level.

Retailers applied both considerable expense and care to the choice of fittings and interior decoration. Goods on display in a shop had their value and fashionable status underlined, or even to an extent created, by the decorations and fittings which surrounded them. Attention to interior design was particularly important for the retailing goldsmiths carrying out bespoke orders. In this case, reassurance of fashion expertise had to be conveyed beyond the stock on show to the retailer's personal trade networking skills. Customers expectations could be fulfilled by appropriate fittings and decoration, but also shaken by inappropriate design. Shop design aimed to frame the goods it sold with a convincing setting, but it was convincing only if there was consistency between the quality of the goods, the type of display, the level of interior decoration and the intended level of customer. Retailing goldsmiths in the early eighteenth century employed display techniques and interior design to a considerable degree and were sophisticated in their deployment of these devices. Design and display were used as sophisticated marketing devices and constituted a crucial element in goldsmiths' retailing strategies.

Comparison with other shops

A comparison of interior design and display in goldsmiths' shops with that of other shops clarifies the specificity of goldsmiths' design within a general retailing context. The image on a trade card used for Martha Cole and Martha Houghton's draper's shop from *c.*1720 (Fig. 50) represents a door ajar and offers a glimpse into the shopkeeper's parlour where special customers would have been invited to sit and relax. Typically a window is represented between the parlour and the shop, allowing the shopkeeper to keep an eye on the shop and the shop staff from the parlour. In addition, this trade card shows features of interior decoration similar to those used by goldsmiths; decorative work around the arched door, an arch into another part of the shop, and the use of drawers to formally present goods to the customer. The trays with ribbons on them seen on the counter would have come from nests of drawers such as those used by goldsmiths for keeping jewellery.

In comparison with other trades however, goldsmiths were exceptional in their use of glass show cases and glass presses. From inventories and images it is clear that other trades would place their goods on display as extensively as goldsmiths — ceramics were displayed on racks, cloth was displayed in bolts on open shelves, unrolled cloth was allowed to flow down from hooks, finished items of clothing were hung up in shops, hats were propped on specially made stands — but these goods were not placed behind glass. The nature of the goldsmiths' fittings specifically reflected and enhanced

Fig. 50. Detail from trade card for Martha Cole and Martha Houghton, drapers, *c*.1720.
(Victoria and Albert Museum)

the valuable nature of the individual items they sold. Glass casing made gold and silverware one step more inaccessible and underlined their special and elite qualities while still keeping them visible. It perhaps also provided a particular air of grandeur to what might be potentially a very expensive single purchase for the customer. And because, in comparison with other trades, high class goldsmiths frequently carried out bespoke orders for customers, it would have been much more important for them to provide a distinct visual expression of their credit worthiness than for those trades selling from current stock. When retailing goldsmiths also acted as bankers, this external expression of their personal financial standing, in what was the public front to the banking business, was even more important and significant.[16]

While drapers and china sellers did not employ expensive glass cases, they did, however, have other furnishings in their shops which goldsmiths did not commonly employ, such as mirrors, pictures and tables, which sought to create a comfortable and attractive interior. There is a mirror prominently positioned in Martha Cole's trade

---

[16] This point is an important key to high-class goldsmiths' shop design and needs to be developed further. Its relevance became clear from Stephen Quinn's paper on goldsmith bankers and I am grateful to him for highlighting and discussing the significance of it.

card (Fig. 50). In William Marford's draper's shop, inventoried in 1721, there were a 'pier glasse and 3 glass sconces, 4 leather stools, 2 chairs and cushions, a silk curtain and 10 indian pictures'.[17] Henry Ackerman's china shop was inventoried in 1723 and included '6 Cain Chairs a painted card Table ... a Looking Glass a pair of Glass Sconces 4 pair of Glass scales...the Counters, Shelves Drawers & Racks'.[18]

The lamps, candlesticks and sconces which appear in profusion in inventories from other trades, do not appear in any of the goldsmiths' inventories. Selling by daylight had been an early ordinance of the Goldsmiths' Company to guard against possible fraud. While goldsmiths of the eighteenth century no longer needed to adhere to this regulation, retailing by natural light would have been a mark of honest dealing with the customer that was so important to establish in the goldsmith's trade.

Drapers and china sellers used a profusion of light sources to create an attractive ambience. Lit during the day as well as at night, these lamps, candlesticks and sconces would have reflected their light in the mirrors around the walls of the shop. A visiting Frenchman commented in 1755:

> These shops they make as deep as possibly they can; the further end is generally lighted from above, a kind of illumination which, joined to the glasses, the sconces and the rest of the furniture ... is frequently productive of a theatrical effect, of a most agreeable vista.[19]

In comparison with the goldsmiths, wealthy drapers and china sellers tended to place a premium on comfortable and attractive furnishings rather than on display fittings, and expensive glass cases may have been seen as inappropriate for these types of goods. Drapers and china sellers sought to achieve the lavish and enticing interior that was achieved by goldsmiths with their use of glass, through the ambience of the shop. And although individual china and drapery items were less valuable than items of gold or silverware, there was no reason for the fitting up of a china shop to be less carefully designed than that of a goldsmith's. The furnishings of Henry Ackerman the china seller were valued in 1723 at £30. 5s. 0d., which was four pounds more than the most expensive goldsmith's fittings found among the Orphans Court inventories: those of Michael Wilson, which were valued at £26. 5s. 0d. in 1709.[20]

Display and decoration were important tools for eighteenth-century retailers across the board. An appealing, attractive and attentive interior with chairs, tables, and obliging shop staff were devices crucial to detain the customer, to sit them down and to sell to them. This could be achieved through an air of grandeur and wealth as in goldsmiths' shops, or through an air of luxurious comfort in high class drapers and china sellers. In their turn the fittings, furnishings and decoration made shopping a pleasurable and diverse experience for the consumer. It offered them a secluded and attractive environment in which to consider goods. Visual access to goods, visual enticement and the pleasure of shopping were prime features of the way eighteenth-century shops operated.

---

[17] CLRO, Orph. Inv. 3178.
[18] CLRO, Orph. Inv. 3157.
[19] Jean Andre Rouquet, *The Present State of the Arts in England* (ed R W Lightbown; London, 1970), p. 11.
[20] CLRO, Orph. Inv. 3157, Henry Ackerman; CLRO Orph. Inv. 2856, Michael Wilson.

By using the techniques of design and display, retailing goldsmiths were conforming to the procedures of retailing in general. Each trade used different methods of display depending on how the particular qualities of the goods they sold were best promoted. But each trade was drawing on a body of common knowledge and range of common techniques for the task of selling. Retailers had far more in common with each other across trades than they did with the tasks of producing within their own trade. In the 1570s it was stated that: 'A merchant cannot be a retailer for want of skill and acquaintance with customers, which requires an apprenticeship to bring them into it'.[21] Part of the skill of retailing was being able to exploit the marketing potential of the sales environment.

The Business Identity of Shops

In her study of the retailing goldsmiths Parker and Wakelin, Helen Clifford shows that over three quarters of the silverware that Parker and Wakelin sold came in special orders from account clients and that these orders were more elaborate and expensive than the wares on sale in the shop.[22] In this case, what relevance would display and decoration within the shop have had to these more lucrative customers who need not necessarily even have entered the shop to make their purchase?

Daniel Defoe was quite clear that the indications of a successful shop were 'well-filled presses and shelves, and the great choice of rich and fashionable goods'.[23] It was this that would draw custom and it was this that was the mark of the reputation or 'credit', as Defoe termed it, of the shopkeeper. Both exterior and interior design and the way stock was displayed were the external manifestations of a successful business. They signified all the attendant qualities a successful business would have to offer the consumer; the provision of long term credit, attentive and informed advice, efficient and speedy service, skill in the selection of suppliers, and access to fashionable designs. And these were qualities particularly important for courting account customers. The success of the shop was based on its reputation for a good stock and good service, and the appearance of the shop was a visual expression of this reputation and formed its business identity.

Francis Place's motive for the expensive fitting up of his first shop in 1799 was 'to have the appearance of means to do business in good style'. As a tailor he did not need a shop in order to trade, he could take work into his home. However, in order to upgrade his business and increase his income he needed to have a business front with the right social connotations to establish him with the social level of clientele he aimed to attract. Within two years, Place explains: 'The customers I had before we came to Charing Cross had all left us, and our new customers were gentlemen who would not deal with a man in a garrett...' Spending over three hundred pounds on a lavish shop window and

---

[21] Calender of State Papers, Domestic, Addenda 1566–79 p. 344, quoted in D. Davis, *A History of Shopping* (London, 1966), p. 60.

[22] H. Clifford, 'Parker and Wakelin: The study of an eighteenth century goldsmithing business with particular reference to the Garrard Ledgers 1770-1776', unpublished Ph.D. Thesis, Royal College of Art, 1989.

[23] D. Defoe, *The Complete English Tradesman* (New York, 1970), p. 208.

Fig. 51. Trade card for Abraham Price, wallpaper seller, c.1715.
(British Museum, Heal Collection)

the stock for his second shop in 1801, Place declared that 'display in every way in which it could be made was necessary to enable me to procure as large a share of business as I required.'[24] For a high class shop a strong business identity, through the shop front and interior design, was necessary in order to gain account customers' patronage, even if the customer thereafter only corresponded with the shop. In fact it is

---

[24] Francis Place, manuscript autobiography, British Library, MSS ADD 35, 142–4, pp. 85–123.

probable that account customers often did enter and use the shops they patronised, in particular to seek the advice of the retailer in placing an order.[25]

Account customers appear to have ordered their goods by writing to a shop, rather than to its workshop. Customers corresponded with the business front of the partnership. In Parker and Wakelin's case customers received receipts and bills printed with the logo of the 'King's Arms and Feathers', the image used on the sign outside the shop, for the shop's address, and as the retailer's stamp on goods they sold. When George Wickes set up the 'Kings Arms and Feathers' in 1735 he spent £364. 10s. 2d. on fitting up the shop, employing both painters and carvers.

In the nineteenth century shops increasingly sold branded products promoted by the manufacturer, and it was through the manufacturer's advertising that consumers became informed about products. But in the eighteenth century promotion by manufacturers was limited to patent products which might be advertised in newspapers. The use of newspaper advertising by shops in the eighteenth century, however, was very limited, even in the later part of the century when newspaper circulation increased.[26] Trade cards and handbills were far more numerous and influential than newspaper advertisements for shop promotion, and when retailers used trade cards as advertisements it was to emphasise their particular shop in the mind of the consumer, rather than any particular branded goods (Fig. 51). The design of the shop, its shop front and interior decoration, was the prime means whereby consumers were drawn into shops and thus was the prime means by which they were introduced to goods. It was the shop itself which was the prime means of advertising for retailers in the eighteenth century. Despite the absence of widespread newspaper distribution in the early eighteenth century, marketing, through the shop, played a crucial role in the promotion and sale of goods. In the eighteenth century it was, in a sense, the shop which was branded rather than the goods it sold.

Down-market Selling

In an engraving from the 1740s or 1750s called 'The Tinware Dealer' (Fig. 52) a 'bulk' or wooden lock-up shop of the simplest kind is depicted, one half of its front flaps down to form a counter and the other up to form an awning. These flaps were battened down at the end of the day forming a secure store for the goods being sold.[27] Despite the simplicity of the shop, the display the tinware dealer puts on is impressive. Not only is the quantity and range of goods on show extensive and eye-catching to the casual passer-by, the goods are also very immediate — literally just an arm's reach away. Even shops lower down the market in the eighteenth century made the most of their chance to display their goods. But such shops could not detain their customers or

---

[25] This is evident, for example, in the goldsmith Joseph Brasbridge's autobiography, *The Fruits of Experience* (2nd edn.; London, 1824).

[26] Four different newspapers from the Burney Collection at the British Library were assessed at ten-year intervals from 1720–1790.

[27] During the seventeenth century, the Goldsmiths' Company regularly searched in the St. Bartholomew Day and Southwark Fairs for sub-standard wares sold by goldsmiths or lotterymen, presumably from smaller lock-ups of this sort. (Editor's note)

Fig. 52. Engraving after a painting by Killian 'The Tinware Dealer', 1740s or 1750s.
(Victoria and Albert Museum)

articulate the setting for their goods in the same way as more permanent shops, which offered seclusion from the street for both the buyer and the seller. However, display was clearly still of prime importance even for down market retailers.

Larger down-market shops with permanent sites are a slightly different matter, and evidence for these comes primarily from newspaper advertisements. While advertisements placed by shops in the eighteenth century were extremely limited, a small number of shops advertised on a regular, often weekly basis over a number of years, sometimes decades. From the metalworking trade Briscoes is a good example of this kind of shop (Fig 53). These shops appear to have had a particular trading principle; their advertisements suggest a very large stock made up of a large range of goods of a standardised nature, and, specifically, what they offered the consumer were finished goods. Most offered secondhand plate as well as new goods that were 'kept ready finished'. One of these large scale shops advertised twenty thousand ounces of 'ready finished' silver and quoted the goods at standard weights in its trade card.[28]

For the consumer the attraction of these shops must have been fourfold: the chance for customers to see and compare the finished product before they bought, instant purchase with no waiting for an order to be made up, a vast choice of goods on offer and, finally, low prices. The advertisements stated frequently that they sold 'at the

[28] Thomas Daniell's trade card quoted in Clifford, 'Parker and Wakelin'.

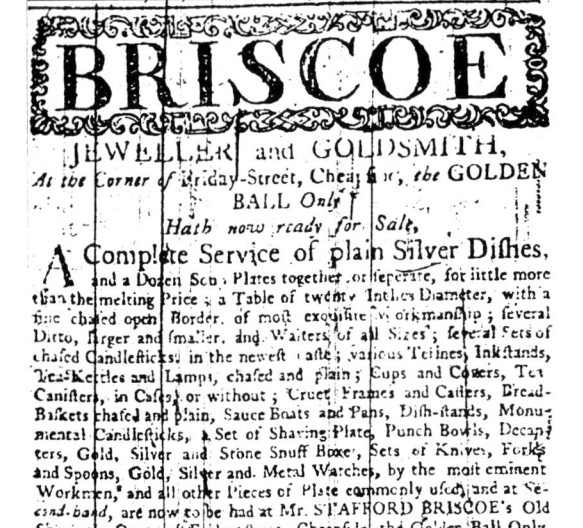

Fig. 53. Newspaper advertisement for Briscoe, goldsmith and jeweller, from *The General Advertiser*, 2 January 1750.

(British Library, Burney Collection)

lowest prices for ready Money'. Stipulations of cash sales only, without any possibility of credit for the customer, allowed the retailer to keep prices down. Unlike the high class goldsmiths, whose profit came from special orders, the profits of these retailers came from the high turnover of competitively priced goods. These retailers with their large shops must have employed a different sales method from that of the high class goldsmiths. It seems likely that along with cash sales went fixed prices for goods. The usual procedure of haggling over prices was a time consuming and skilled business requiring close supervision of any staff by the shopkeeper. For these large shops, needing a high turnover and a quick through put of customers, fixed prices would have been one way of speeding up the sales process and it would have been much more effective in a large establishment with large numbers of staff.

More specific evidence of large scale, quick through-put selling comes from the drapers' trade. The sales procedure of a draper's shop on Old London Bridge in the 1780s was recorded by Robert Owen:

> Not much time was allowed for bargaining, a price being fixed for everything, and, compared with other houses, cheap. If any demur was made, or much hesitation, the article asked for was withdrawn, and, as the shop was generally full from morning till late in the evening, another customer was attended to.[29]

Such sales methods aimed to clinch a sale quickly and to reduce the amount of time shop staff spent in contact with the customer. They represent a specialised form of selling and such firms as Briscoes may have reaped as great a profit as the highest class bespoke goldsmith.

In terms of design, these establishments seemed to have had a large ground plan with less emphasis on elaborate interior design than bespoke goldsmiths and a particular emphasis on the display of goods, especially in terms of quantity and variety. Display must have taken on a new significance as: firstly, these shops would have been much more dependent on attracting passing trade; secondly, one of the attractions of these

---

[29] Robert Owen, *The Life of Robert Owen Written By Himself* (London, 1971), p. 13.

shops was the opportunity for customers to see and compare the final product before they bought it; thirdly, with a fast selling system, display would have been privileged over service and skilled advice. In comparison with other shops the task of decision-making was placed fully on the unaided customer. But for the customer such shops offered choice, personal selection, cheap prices and quick, no frills selling.

These features were signalled by the design of the shop. Rather than extensive and elaborate interior decoration, this sales method is reflected in shop inventories by large numbers of serviceable counters and simple display fittings together with a large and extremely high value of stock.[30] The design of these shops, with their emphasis on accessible display, was tuned to signal competitive pricing and slick selling. Here different sales methods lead to different methods of design and display and a different public profile for the shop. Design and display can clearly be seen to have been key aspects of selling in all trades and at all levels of the market in the first half of the eighteenth century.

Various marketing techniques were open to retailers in the eighteenth century, the most important of these were shop design and display. Amongst retailers of the early eighteenth century high class goldsmiths provided some of the most lavish and impressive shop interiors. These interiors were geared specifically to the particular sales requirement of the goldsmiths wares and to a particular market level, and they were geared to promoting the standing of the retailer and his or her business. Large-scale retailers of gold and silverware likewise used display to sell their goods and interior design to promote their particular sales features of extensive choice and competitive pricing. It seems that such marketing techniques were most probably also in use before the eighteenth century — Daniel Defoe complained at the lengths such devices were taken to in 1727, but not that design and display were new retailing techniques.

---

[30] For example, CLRO, Orph. Inv. 3102, Moses Read, draper.

The goldsmiths and the London luxury trades, 1550 to 1750

JOHN STYLES

It is appropriate that a collection of essays concerned with questions of innovation should itself represent a significant innovation in the study of early-modern material culture. The collection's novelty lies both in its subject matter and its approach. The luxury trades of early modern London have been unjustifiably neglected by historians of manufacturing, business and technology in the period. They have customarily identified provincial England as the site of the most exciting developments, whether they be the rise of rural manufacturing in the seventeenth century, or the emergence of the factory in the eighteenth. The energetic efforts of scholars working within a decorative arts framework have ensured that the London goldsmiths' trade, the quintessential luxury trade, has suffered less neglect than some other London-based luxury manufactures of the period. But the orientation of much existing work on goldsmiths and their products is towards the long-established connoisseurial concerns of attribution and dating. This collection of essays breaks new ground by addressing the whole range of goldsmiths' activities, from the technique and forms of organisation that sustained their manufacture of fine silver objects to their role as innovators in retailing and banking. To achieve this breadth of focus, the contributors to the collection combine the methods of artefact-based scholarship and manuscript-based scholarship in a fruitful partnership, which draws on the best existing work in the field and can stand as a model for future research.

The collection's findings regarding innovation and skill in goldsmiths' work in London in the early modern period are, of course, of primary significance for the history of the trade itself and the study of its surviving products. Each of the essays dealing with London goldsmiths establishes its own relationship to existing work on the trade. The two essays on aspects of goldsmiths' practice in continental Europe serve to locate the London goldsmiths in their international context. But there is another context in which the findings of the essays in this collection should be assessed. Given the scholarly neglect which the London luxury trades of the seventeenth and eighteenth centuries have suffered, the important implications of these essays for the wider history of the luxury trades need to be established and identified. That is the task of this concluding chapter.

The goldsmiths were, of course, distinctive in a number of important respects. Campbell in his *London Tradesman* of 1747 picked out the goldsmith's employment as 'the most genteel of any in the mechanic way', while the activities of significant numbers of goldsmiths as bankers in the seventeenth century had no real equivalent among the other London manufacturing trades.[1] But many of the innovations in product,

---

[1] R. Campbell, *The London Tradesman* (London, 1747), p. 142.

skill, and organisation that characterised the goldsmiths did have parallels in the other trades of the period. It is important to consider such parallels in order to clarify the extent to which these innovations were the outcome of developments peculiar to the goldsmiths and the extent to which they arose from influences that bore on the luxury sector as a whole. Three issues in particular will be addressed here — the organisation of production, the means by which design information was communicated, and innovation in form and ornament.

Consider first the organisation of production. As far as the role of the livery Companies is concerned, the pattern that emerges from study of the goldsmiths is reproduced in manufacturing trade after manufacturing trade — an almost complete retreat from efforts to control product innovation, the organisation of production and the content of training. This is not to say that the Companies were entirely inactive. The development by some Livery Companies of their role as parliamentary lobbyists in response to the increased flow of legislation after the Glorious Revolution of 1688 demonstrates that they could retain an influence on the fortunes of their trades that went beyond their continuing ceremonial, social and municipal functions.[2] Nevertheless, in contrast to the experience of a comparable continental city like Paris, the Companies' capacity to organise and regulate their trades was severely constrained, particularly after the mid seventeenth century. Although it has been argued that in eighteenth-century Paris guild restrictions did not prevent innovations in the organisation of manufacturing, the weakness of corporate controls in London undoubtedly facilitated a number of striking organisational changes which characterised not only the goldsmiths but a host of other trades. Prominent among these was the relatively uninhibited development of the division of labour through functional and product specialisation, subcontracting and the dispersal of some production processes to the provinces.[3]

The discovery of these forms of division of labour has presented a powerful challenge to the received image of the goldsmith's trade. In the past, much of the study of fine silver was undertaken in terms of the marker's mark. The result was an analysis of style and technique that was essentially biographical. It privileged the individual genius of the master craftsman and the integrity of his workshop as a manufacturing unit. The revelation that subcontracting was widespread in the trade, that particular makers specialised in particular products, and that specialist retailers simply overstruck the marks of their suppliers has required a radical rethinking of who was responsible for stylistic and technical initiative in the making of fine silver. Yet divided labour of this kind was common in the London luxury trades, and in some cases was more extensive than among the goldsmiths. Coachmaking was a trade with an even more socially exclusive clientele than goldsmithing and one that emerged on any scale only in the period covered by this book. It involved the assembly of a finished vehicle from a

[2] L. Davison, T. Hitchcock, T. Kiern and R.B. Shoemaker (eds.), *Stilling the Grumbling Hive. The Response to Social and Economic Problems in England, 1689–1750* (Stroud, 1992), p. xxxiv.

[3] See, for different views of the restrictions on business organisation imposed by the Paris guilds in the eighteenth century, M. Sonenscher, *Work and Wages. Natural Law, Politics and the Eighteenth-Century French Trades* (Cambridge, 1989), pp. 210–43 and C. Fairchilds, 'Populuxe goods in eighteenth-century Paris', in J. Brewer and R. Porter (eds.), *Consumption and the World of Goods in the Seventeenth and Eighteenth Centuries* (London, 1993), p. 232.

great diversity of component parts, some of which were themselves sub-assemblies of other parts — wheels of wood and iron, harness of leather and iron, linings made of various textiles, carved decorative wood, glass windows, cast ornamental metal. Coachmakers owned workshops which often doubled as retail premises. By the eighteenth century these workshops were concentrated on Long Acre in Covent Garden. Nevertheless, as Andrew Federer has pointed out, 'a master coachmaker was as much a co-ordinator of subcontracting smiths, wheelwrights, coachpainters, saddlers, carvers and others as the supervisor of an artisan workshop.'[4] Final assembly of the component parts may have taken place within the master coachmaker's workshop, but the parts themselves were often made and assembled to order by independent businesses in other parts of the metropolitan area. By the mid eighteenth century, of course, goldsmiths were beginning to subcontract work not only within the London area, but far beyond it, drawing on the specialist skills of manufacturers in Birmingham and Sheffield. Yet in doing so, they were following a path trodden by other luxury businesses, such as drapers, cutlers and hatters, who increasingly became specialist retailers of finished goods produced in the provinces by independent manufacturers or tied manufacturing agents.[5]

The reasons for the growth of subcontracting and functional and product specialisation across so many trades were various. Given that the population of London grew from approximately 80,000 in 1550 to 675,000 in 1750, these developments can be regarded as, in the broadest terms, an instance of the tendency for the division of labour to intensify as the size of the market increases, a phenomenon which was identified by a number of seventeenth- and eighteenth-century commentators on economics, including Adam Smith. From the point of view of those masters who subcontracted work to others, the most immediately obvious benefit of subcontracting was the access it provided to specialisms that were not required frequently enough to justify employment of a full-time skilled journeyman in the master's workshop. It enabled masters to limit their own manufacturing activities or even to become pure retailers, while still handling a wide range of product types. Between the mid sixteenth and the mid eighteenth century the London metropolitan area became in effect a vast and diverse industrial district,[6] with an exceptionally high density of skilled workers in an unprecedented range of trades, linked through criss-crossing networks of subcontracting and piecework. These networks provided masters in the luxury trades with a means to secure ever more minutely defined specialist skills as they required them. The growth of subcontracting and specialisation along these lines was one of the crucial ways by which London was transformed over the two centuries covered by this book into a centre of luxury production capable of performing in most trades to the

[4] A. Federer, 'Payment, credit and the organisation of work in eighteenth-century Westminster', unpublished paper presented to the SSRC Conference on Manufacture in Town and Country before the Factory, Oxford, 1980, p. 11.

[5] For drapers, see Campbell, *London Tradesman*, pp. 194–7, though he exaggerates the extent to which it was normal for cloth to be dyed and finished in London; for cutlers, see Campbell, *London Tradesman*, pp. 238–9; for hatters, see D. Corner, 'The Tyranny of Fashion: the case of the felt-hatting trade in the late seventeenth and eighteenth centuries', *Textile History*, 22 (1991), pp. 153–78.

[6] The term is Alfred Marshall's and was used by him to describe the interconnected nature of manufacturing among the medium and small firms of nineteenth-century Sheffield and Lancashire. See his *Industry and Trade* (London, 1919), pp. 283–8.

highest western European standards of technique and aesthetic quality, broadly at the same level as, for example, Paris or Amsterdam. Campbell recognised this when he remarked that:

> the goldsmith employs several distinct workmen, almost as many as there are different articles in his shop; for in this great city there are hands that excel in every branch, and are constantly employed but in that one of which they are masters. This gives us an advantage over many foreign nations in this article, as they are obliged to employ the same hand in every branch of the trade, and it is impossible to expect that a man employed in such an infinite variety can finish his work to any perfection, at least, not so much as he who is constantly employed in one thing.[7]

But there were other reasons for the proliferation of subcontracting and specialisation. High rents in the fashionable shopping streets of London made subcontracting production to workshops in cheaper locations an attractive option. Perhaps even more important was, as Federer has argued, the inescapable pressure on all those involved in the luxury trades to achieve a satisfactory balance between the supply of trade credit to customers and payment to workers.[8] Producers of luxury goods had little choice but to extend long credit to their customers. Campbell repeatedly protested against the reluctance of wealthy customers to pay their bills promptly. He complained that tailors who furnished gentlemen 'would raise Estates soon, were it not for the delays in payment among the Quality', that 'the Gentry are no more solicitous about paying their Saddler than any other Tradesmen', and that coachmakers 'deal with none but Nobility and Quality, and according to their Mode must trust a long Time, and sometimes may happen never to be paid'. His complaints were echoed by many other seventeenth- and eighteenth-century commentators.[9] While luxury tradesmen had to wait months or even years to be paid, they were obliged to pay their journeymen regular weekly wages in cash. In most London trades journeymen employed in the master's workshop appear to have been paid in cash on a more or less regular weekly basis. Because few luxury businesses enjoyed ready access to liquidity, masters in the luxury trades faced a constant struggle to reconcile delayed payment for their products with regular cash payments to their journeymen.[10] Subcontracting offered a welcome escape from this predicament because it was customary to oblige firms or individuals to whom work was put out at piece rates to wait long periods for payment.

That escape was acquired at a price. Subcontracted work was usually more expensive than work undertaken for day rates in the workshop. It could pose problems with regard to quality, because direct supervision of the way the work was undertaken was more difficult if it was in the hands of subcontractors. Delivery of work on time could be a problem because those who undertook subcontracted work had their own pressing priorities when it came to scheduling which might not coincide with those who put out the work to them. Problems of quality and delivery were particularly acute in the case of fashion goods

---

[7] Campbell, *London Tradesman*, p. 142.
[8] The following discusion is based on Federer, 'Payment, credit and the organisation of work in eighteenth-century Westminster'.
[9] Campbell, *London Tradesman*, pp.194, 234, 230. For other contemporary comments see P. Earle, *The Making of the English Middle Class* (London, 1989), pp. 116–7.
[10] Earle, *Making of the English Middle Class,* pp. 117–23.

that had to be sold quickly or not at all, goods made from precious, easily damaged materials and goods manufactured by provincial subcontractors over whom supervision was at its most tenuous. Considerations of these kinds can help explain the particular patterns of subcontracting characteristic of the goldsmiths by the mid eighteenth century. Plate, jewellery and other goldsmiths' wares were extremely expensive, bespoke products with a high visual design content. It is not surprising, therefore, that subcontracting took place mainly within London, where lines of supervision and flows of visual information were not too extended. London goldsmiths looked to Sheffield or Birmingham only for certain specialities, such as Sheffield plate.[11] Fashionable London hatters, by contrast, much of whose work was not bespoke, increasingly subcontracted a large proportion of it to Lancashire and Cheshire as the eighteenth century progressed.[12] Some fashionable West End tailors, on the other hand, appear not to have subcontracted at all, perhaps because theirs was a bespoke trade using very expensive and easily spoiled materials. These materials, like the silver worked by the goldsmith, were often the property of the customer, but, unlike silver, could not be melted down and reworked. The costs that could arise from spoiling cloth and accessories certainly put a premium on close supervision and therefore probably discouraged subcontracting.[13] Tailors and salesmen at the less fashionable end of the market, producing both ready-made and bespoke garments from cheaper material they owned themselves, had no such inhibitions.[14]

The ability to provide customers with appropriate, fashionable designs was crucial to the successful marketing of fine goldsmiths' ware. Goldsmiths had to be able to secure information about design, to initiate or at least to adapt designs when customers required and to ensure that those who executed the work, whether they be journeymen or subcontractors, did so to the required design specification. It is for this reason that Campbell recommended in 1747 that the goldsmith, 'ought to be a good designer' and that 'designing is the chief part of his early study, previous to his apprenticeship.'[15] Like most who used the word during the first half of the eighteenth century, what Campbell meant by designing was the ability to produce drawings on paper that could subsequently be executed in three dimensions. Even at the highest levels in the trade, this did not imply that goldsmiths should necessarily generate entirely original designs. Much of their design work was expected to involve the interpretation and adaptation of designs that already existed, whether on paper or as objects.

It is not surprising, therefore, that sixteenth-century goldsmiths were one of the first London trades to make extensive use of printed design information in the form of engravings.[16] This was a development of immense significance for the London luxury

[11] H. Clifford, 'Parker and Wakelin: a Westminster firm of goldsmiths in the later eighteenth century' (Ph.D. Thesis, Royal College of Art, 1989), chapter 4.
[12] Corner, 'The tyranny of fashion'.
[13] Federer, 'Payment, credit and the organisation of work in eighteenth-century Westminster'.
[14] See, for example, Public Record Office, 133/114/38, Exchequer Depositions, Smith v. Goater, 1745. I would like to thank Andrew Federer for bringing my attention to this case.
[15] Campbell, *London Tradesman*, p. 142.
[16] It has, of course, been argued that the practice of making prints on paper as patterns to copy originated within the goldsmiths' trade in continental Europe; see S. Lambert (ed), *Pattern and Design. Designs for the Decorative Arts, 1480–1980* (London, 1983), p. 2 and, for the whole issue of design for English silver in the period, P. Glanville, *Silver in Tudor and Early Stuart England* (London 1990), chapter 8.

trades, because in the course of the next two centuries most of them would come to rely more and more on printed designs to determine the form and ornament of an ever-expanding range of artefacts. Before the mid seventeenth century, design engravings came overwhelmingly from continental Europe, particularly France, Germany and the Low Countries, mainly in the form of loose sheets of engraved ornament not intended solely for goldsmiths.[17] Continental engravings were sometimes reprinted in London, but it was only from the Restoration that engraved ornament of this kind began to be originated there. By that date, the supply of printed ornament had become the preserve of specialist London dealers. The crucial importance of goldsmiths and associated tradespeople as customers to these specialists is demonstrated by their prominent place in a 1666 advertisement by the bookseller and print dealer Robert Walton, who described his stock as 'extraordinarily useful for goldsmiths, jewellers, chasers, gravers, painters, carvers, drawers, needlewomen and all handicrafts.'[18]

Goldsmiths may have been precocious in their use of printed ornament, but they were not unique. One of the most striking new features of seventeenth- and eighteenth-century manufacturing in London was a dramatic increase in the use of two-dimensional paper plans for subsequent three-dimensional execution. Not only did pre-existing forms of production like architecture, embroidery and carving come to rely increasingly on printed designs, but the demand for printed design information was reinforced by the arrival of new manufactures reliant on sophisticated design and ornament, such as cabinetmaking, coachmaking, cotton printing, silkweaving and lacquering. The consequence was a vastly increased use of both printed and hand-drawn two-dimensional designs in the making of luxury goods, designs which were employed for a variety of purposes. They were used as sources of visual ideas, as instructions for the execution of the work, as records of information about products, and as a means of visualising products for customers.

The London book and print trade responded to this expanding market for two-dimensional design among the manufacturing trades with prints and pattern books. At first, as has been pointed out, most of these originated on the continent and consisted of decorative ornament that could be executed in a variety of media, testimony to the extent to which the luxury trades participated in a common decorative culture, which stylistically was classical and international. From the late seventeenth century, however, prints and books of this kind increasingly were originated in London and targeted at particular trades. This was true of engraved designs for silver, but to a lesser extent than designs for other types of artefact, particularly furniture. Engraved designs for silver by Englishmen remained extremely rare before the final third of the eighteenth century and, in contrast to furniture, it was particularly unusual for English publishers to produce printed images of whole silver objects.[19] Moreover, one of the most famous exceptions, Smith and Linnell's *A New Book of Ornaments Useful for Silver-Smith's Etc.*, published in the late 1750s, is better interpreted as a

---

[17] P. Glanville, *Silver in England* (London, 1987), p. 226.
[18] Quoted in L. Rostenberg, *English Publishers in the Graphic Arts* (New York, 1963), p. 45.
[19] The principal exceptions are the prints published by C. de Moelder in London in 1694 and Smith and Linnell's *A New Book of Ornaments Useful for Silver-Smiths Etc.* of the later 1750s. On this issue, see Glanville, *Silver in England*, p. 242.

demonstration of virtuosity in Rococo design and engraving than as a serious design source for silver plate. Essentially a caprice, few of its extreme and eccentric designs appear to have been executed at the time.[20]

Perhaps the rarity of English engraved design for silver can be explained by the facts that stylistic innovation in the London goldsmiths' trade before 1750 came principally from overseas and the key agents of change were immigrant craftsmen and their offspring. It was for continental engraved ornament that there was the greatest demand and it was predominantly Dutch, German and French immigrants who initiated design and technical innovation in the making of fine silver. The very presence of significant numbers of immigrant craftsmen operating at the highest level in the trade may itself have limited the demand for London-originated engraved design. Immigrants were, of course, vitally important in a number of other seventeenth- and early eighteenth-century luxury trades, most notably silkweaving, but there were also trades where they played a more muted role. The manufacture of fine furniture, which spawned a good deal of London-originated engraved design, especially in the 1740s and 1750s, was one of these. The predominance among engraved designs for silver (whether of English or continental origin) of ornament over whole objects may reflect the relative importance of ornament as opposed to form in the making of fine plate, at least before the emergence of neoclassicism. Certainly when Campbell discussed the role of design in goldsmiths' training, it was in the context of making moulds for those cast decorative components which were such a significant and innovatory feature of late seventeenth- and early eighteenth-century silver.[21]

The appetite among London goldsmiths for engraved ornament is evidence that those who bought their goods were keenly attuned to the appearance of their purchases. Visual novelty and fashion played an important part in shaping the market for fine silver and, as had been pointed out, for most of the period covered by this book the principal sources of innovation were overseas. Indeed, it has been possible to write much of the history of fine English silver in this period in terms of the impact of successive waves of fashionable continental style. Silver lent itself to refashioning. In contrast to luxury durables made from wood or clay, silver objects could be melted down and re-manufactured to conform to fashionable taste, while retaining their intrinsic bullion value. Nevertheless, some caution is required regarding the relationship between fashionability, design and product innovation.

Fine silver was a fashion product, in the sense that its successful sale depended on its appearance conforming to current metropolitan and international notions of what was stylish and up-to-date. However, the term 'fashion' is a ambiguous one, which has been used by historians to mean everything from visual novelty of almost any kind to the very precise annual shifts which had become characteristic of metropolitan high style in clothing by the early eighteenth century. For all its capacity to be melted down and reworked, the cycle of visual innovation in fine silver spread over several years, resembling in this respect furniture and interior design much more than clothing. It was the jeweller, not the goldsmith, whom Campbell identified in his discussion of

---

[20] Lambert, *Pattern and Design*, p. 68.
[21] Campbell, *London Tradesman*, p. 143.

goldsmithing and associated trades as requiring an aptitude for fashion and novelty. He wrote that the jeweller, whose products, like clothes, were to be worn, needed:

> a quick invention for new patterns, not only to range the stones in such manner as to give lustre to one another, but to create trade; for a new fashion takes as much with the ladies in jewels as anything else: he that can furnish them oftenest with the newest whim has the best chance for their custom.[22]

Like most luxury artefacts of the period, fashionability in fine silver was a matter of both form and ornament. But the relationship between the two was not necessarily consistent. In the sixteenth and early seventeenth centuries, for example, innovation in fine silver was predominantly a matter of ornament rather than form.[23] It is important to bear in mind in this context that the impact of innovative designs for ornament was longer lasting than the everyday modern use of the notion of fashion might imply. Once in circulation in printed form, ornament for silver could enjoy an extended working life. As Philippa Glanville has pointed out, Stefano della Bella's plates of ornament continued in use in England and elsewhere for a century and a half after they were produced between 1620 and 1664.[24] Within a decorative culture that remained broadly classical for three centuries, it was possible for sources of printed ornament to be used over and over again and on a variety of objects. Ornamental elements were copied and adapted in endless permutations that could transcend particular fashionable styles and particular materials.

As with other luxury goods, innovations in form tended to be less frequent than innovations in ornament. Nevertheless, the period as a whole saw the visual transformation of existing categories of plate and the introduction of many entirely new categories of silver object. Important innovations were objects associated with eating and drinking, like tea equipages, tureens and cruets, and also objects that formed matching sets, such as toilet services. This proliferation of new forms and new products, especially from the mid seventeenth century, was characteristic of elite material culture as a whole. It can be observed in a variety of materials, for example the tea wares that were manufactured in various ceramics, or new types of furniture, such as tea tables, upholstered chairs and writing desks. These kinds of product innovation were particularly associated with the spread among European elites of French modes of polite refinement in eating and the use of domestic space, and of artefacts and groceries from outside Europe, particularly Asia. The general tendency towards product innovation was certainly no more marked for silver than it was for other luxury goods.

Between 1550 and 1750, many of the patterns of innovation in product, skill, and organisation that characterised the London goldsmiths were broadly reproduced in the other London luxury trades. This is hardly surprising. One of the most striking features of the economic history of England in this period is an overall shift away from the import of manufactured goods and towards their export. London's luxury manufactures shared in this process. Their experience for most of the period under discussion was one of

---

[22] Campbell, *London Tradesman*, p. 142.

[23] For the chronology of foreign influence on form as opposed to ornament, see Glanville, *Silver in England*, p. 226.

[24] Glanville, *Silver in England*, p. 236 and for the longevity of le Pautre's designs, see ibid., p. 240.

progressive import substitution — the domestic market for imported foreign luxury manufactures was captured by their London-made equivalents. The unifying tendency of this shared economic experience was reinforced by the fact that the luxury trades operated in the same rapidly-growing metropolis, enjoyed similar opportunities for extending the division of labour, employed roughly equivalent levels of hand technology, and partook of a common decorative culture, which stylistically was broadly classical and international. Nevertheless, this examination of just a few aspects of the goldsmiths' trade has served to demonstrate that in a number of important ways it was distinctive. Further exploration of these patterns of similarity and difference is essential in order to refine historical understanding not only of the goldsmiths' trade, but also of the still-obscure history of London luxury manufacturing as a whole.